INTELLIGENT INTERACTIONS

PRACTICAL GUIDE TO PROFITABLE CUSTOMER EXPERIENCE

JASON MILLER

Copyright © 2014 Jason Miller

First Edition

All rights reserved.

No part of this publication may be reproduced, stored in a retrieval system or transmitted in any form or by any means, electronic, mechanical, photocopying, recording, scanning or otherwise, except under the terms of the Copyright, Designs and Patents Act 1988 or under the terms of a license issued by the Copyright Licensing Agency Ltd.

ISBN-13: 978-1494997106

Book Cover & Design by PIXEL eMarketing INC.

Legal Disclaimer

The publisher and the author make no representations or warranties with respect to the accuracy or completeness of the contents of this work and specifically disclaim all warranties, including without limitation warranties for a particular purpose. No warranty may be created or extended by sales or promotional materials. The advice and strategies contained herein may not be suitable for every situation.

Neither the publisher nor the author shall be liable for damages arising herefrom. The fact that an organization or website is referred to in this work as a citation and/or a potential source of further information does not mean that the author or the publisher endorses the information the organization or website may provide or recommendations it may make.

Further, readers should be aware that Internet websites listed in this work may have changed or disappeared between when this work was written and when it is read.

This book is dedicated to:
My Mother, My Family, and My Friends.
They are my most important assets. I also dedicate this to any company looking to maximize their most important asset, their customer base.

Contents

Introduction: Real Time Interaction Management 1
   What are these companies doing differently? 3

Part I: Are You Getting the Most Out of Every Customer Interaction? 9

Chapter 1: Defining RTIM as a Business Capability 11
   What Is Real Time Interaction Management? 12
   Customer Centric Decisioning & Business Process Management . 13
   Who Uses Real Time Interaction Management 15
   Proof That It Works. 17
   Interactions, Scale, and Expectations. 19
   What Does RTIM Mean for Your Business? 21
   New Perspectives on Sales: The Elephant Story. 23
   The "Burning Platform" 25

Chapter 2: Why Do You Need Real Time Interaction Management? 25
   The Product & Service Centric Business vs.
   The Customer Centric Business 27
   The Culture of Customer Loyalty. 29
   Types of Loyalty / Retention 30
   Functional Silos and the Ideal Customer Experience. 31
   Customer Contact Management 33
   Analytics and Insight for Business Management. 35
   Cross-Functional Interactions and the 5Ps of strategy. 37
   The Rise of Customer Expectations. 38

Part II: Readiness and Preparation: Using the TIPP Approach. 41

Chapter 3: Strategy and Technology Readiness and Preparation 43
   The TIPP Approach: Transforming Your Organization 44
   How Strategy Readiness and Preparation Equate to Results. 47

    How to Assess Current Business Capabilities. 50
    Your Marketplace Comparison 51
    Data Quality and Complexity 54

Chapter 4: Intelligence Readiness and Preparation 59
    How Data Quality and Complexity Result in Intelligence. 60
    Predictive Models and Advanced Analytics. 61
    The Power of Business Rules 62
    The Types of Analytic Models Needed for Interactions 64

Chapter 5: Process Readiness and Preparation 69
    The Current Process Measures and KPIs. 70
    What Gets Measured Gets Done 73
    What Is the State of Business Process? 75
    Creating Cross-Functional Leadership Buy-in. 76
    Interaction Ownership – Targeting Accountable Candidates 78
    ROI: What Is the Business Case for Interaction Management? . . . 78

Chapter 6: People Readiness and Preparation. 83
    RTIM Effectiveness Begins With Leadership Education and
    Commitment to Funding. 84
    Business Transformation and Education 86
    RTIM Capability Ownership Explained 88
    What Drives Your Business Today? 91
    What Are the Biggest Challenges Your Business Is Facing? 93
    Understanding Current Organizational Strategy and Objectives . 94
    Continuous Business Education – A New Way Forward 97

**Part III: Creating TIPP Designed Real-Time Interactions
for Your Business** **101**

Chapter 7: Prioritizing Customer, Agent, and Business 103
    Customer Interaction Lifecycle 104
    Agent Interaction Experience 107
    Business ROI Strategies 107

Chapter 8: Setting Business Expectations 111
    Program and Project Management 101. 112
    Setting Your Business Scope 113
    Formally Establishing and Leveraging Interaction
    Ownership and Sponsorship. 115
    Timing, Resources, and Scheduling. 117

Chapter 9: **Creating Interactions That Align Strategy to Technology** 119
   How to Assess Business Capabilities in Terms of Technology ... 120
   To Buy or to Build? 121
   In-House vs. Vendor Resources–Guidelines for Successful
   Establishment 122
   In-house Build 122
   Vendor Resources 123
   Designing Data to Create Information 124
   Strategic Interactions for RTIM 126

Chapter 10: **Creating Interactions That Align Intelligence to RTIM** 129
   Questions on Channels, Targets, and Tactics 130
   Design Your Opportunities 131
   Creating and Leveraging Information 132
   Customer Insights 134

Chapter 11: **Creating Interactions That Align People to RTIM** . 137
   Incentive Assessment 138
   Training Needs Assessment 139
   Current Rep Environment Assessment 140
   Communication Channels and Frequency 141

Chapter 12: **Creating Interactions That Align Process to RTIM** 143
   Intelligent Business Process 144
   Understanding Differentiated Service Treatment 145
   Future Processes 147

Part IV: TIPP Taking Action: Implementation of RTIM .. 149

Chapter 13: **Strategy and Technology: Implementing Interactions** 151
   Building and Deploying Technology 152
   Implementing Strategy Through RTIM 153

Chapter 14: **Intelligence: Implementing Interactions** 157
   Testing Intelligent Interactions 158
   Business Trials 158
   Working With Dynamic Testing 160
   Establishing Benchmark Measurements 162

    Test Data Preparation 162
    Test Case Design and Execution 162

Chapter 15: **People: Implementing Interactions** 165
    Change Management 101 166
    Communications and Training. 166
    Process and Interaction Compliance 168

Chapter 16: **Process: Implementing Interactions** 171
    Deploying New Processes. 172
    Measuring Processes 173
    Establishing Benchmark Measurements 175

Chapter 17: **Transitioning to Business as Usual** 179
    Making TIPP a Part of Daily Business. 180

Part V: 360 Degree Vision: Sustaining RTIM as a Business Capability 183

Chapter 18: **Strategy and Technology: Engagement and Commitment to RTIM** 185
    Successful Technology and Strategy: Consumed by Process 185
    Successful Process Is Consumed by Aligned People 186

Chapter 19: **Intelligence: Engagement and Commitment to RTIM** 189
    Interaction Business Rules Management 190
    The New Type of Business:
    Resource –Business / Tech/ Analytics 191
    Balancing the Skill Sets 194
    Cross-Functional Visibility and Neutrality. 195

Chapter 20: **People: Engagement and Commitment to RTIM** . . 197
    Interaction Ownership 198
    Incentive Alignment 199
    Cross-Functions and Channels. 200
    Cross-Functional Governance 201

Chapter 21: **Process: Engagement and Commitment to RTIM** . . 203
    Measurements and Observations 204
    On-going Testing and Learning Environment 205
    Demonstrating ROI. 206

    Key Performance Indicators 208
    Forecasting the Future 209

Part VI: Taking the Throne: Optimizing RTIM. 213

Chapter 22: **Interaction Assets. 215**
    Operational Intelligence and Real Time Insights
    to Project the Future. 216
    Creating an Ever Improving System. 217
    Who Owns the Interaction?. 219
    Monitoring and Improving Measurements 220
    Agile Cross Functional Governance. 222

Chapter 23: **Best Practices for Optimization 225**
    Workbenches for Predictive Analytics 226
    Interaction Assets: Doing More With Less 227
    Experimenting With Processes 229
    How Technology Enables the System. 231
    Your Data Infrastructure 232
    Pre-Configured or Automated RTIM Systems. 234
    Being a Service Orientated Platform 235

Conclusion 237

References. 239

About the Author 257

INTRODUCTION
Real Time Interaction Management

The business world is changing. Customer experience is becoming THE most important element in sales. The more brands understand their customers, the better these real time experiences are becoming. You have noticed it already as a customer. Some companies have faded into the background, while others are popping out in Technicolor, winning your hearts and minds with innovative engagement and business processes. We are on the cusp of a business evolution; an evolution that puts the customer at the center of the business. While not all companies have been active in trying to embrace the notion of customer experience engagement, it is clear that those that have made the shift are leading the way in their various industries. What is interesting is that it is not any particular industry that is blazing the trail, but there certainly is a common theme across service providers. Whether banking giants, insurance firms, or chicken sandwich makers, the companies that are putting their customers in the center of their business universe are reaping huge payoffs!

The insurance industry is notoriously drab and boring and brings to mind gaggles of surly men in grey suits declining claims from their frustrated customers. It came as a surprise, then, that customer experience had such a large impact on this insurer's bottom line. USAA Insurance is leading the way in their niche with customer experience management, and their members are more likely to refer friends and family to USAA than any other company.

At a 77% Temkin score,[1] this banking and insurance provider knows that their customers come first. As a result, they received the Customer Experience Index Award of Excellence in 2013. These customer referrals translate to significant chunks of incremental revenue across the board and lower churn rates compared to their competition! It is just incredible, really. It proves that any company can benefit by focusing more on their existing customers.

When you contemplate today's marketplace and the rising expectations of the consumer, you have two types of companies:

1. Those that are taking action and are on the figurative "court" in the marketplace making things happen and focusing on how to delight their customers.
2. Those companies that are still sitting on the sidelines, watching, not sure if or how to take action and get on the figurative "court" in the marketplace.

For those companies taking action, they are finding that the proof is in the numbers. Companies with little or no customer experience focus—let's call them the "sideliners"—often have churn rates that are two to three times greater than companies that are putting in the work and taking action at cracking the nut on positive customer experience—let's call them the "players.".

Maybe you have heard of some of these "players"? Have you stayed in a Marriott hotel lately? The Marriott hotels brand specifically uses data-driven customer insights and real time interaction management systems to give their customers a *unique and personalized experience* when they stay with the brand. In fact, studies show that three out of four Marriott Rewards[2] members *go out of their way* to stay within the Marriott portfolio because of the high levels of value and service that they receive.

---

1 Study Finds USAA Sets Customer Experience Benchmark, https://www.usaa.com/inet/ent_blogs/Blogs?action=blogpost&blogkey=newsroom&postkey=study_finds_usaa_sets_customer&akredirect=true
2 Marriott International Shares Rare Look Into Innovative Next Generation Marketing Strategy, http://news.marriott.com/innovation/

Another star player in the game does business in the highly competitive field of chicken sandwiches. Chick Fil-A was recently voted into one of the top spots in the 2013 Temkin Experience ratings. This fast food company scored the highest for the second straight year, with an overall rating of 82%. The ratings are based on functional, accessible, and emotional areas in customer experience.[3] Chick Fil-A's investment in customer experience translates into a loyal base of consumers with *recurring revenue* that would not even think of getting a chicken sandwich from another chicken sandwich provider.

What are these companies doing differently?

How are they able to align their business operations to focus on their customer in a way that differentiates them from their competition? In the past five to eight years, there have been significant advances in technology that will enable companies to truly have a one-on-one relationship with their customers; technology that not only understands where the customer has been but is smart enough to predict where the customer is going. It is also flexible enough to perform a multitude of actions. Sounds great, right? The key issue is while technology is changing very fast to address just about every business problem, the business operations side, or the "business" model that many companies swear by, has not changed in a long time. They are comfortable doing the same things they have always done. As time rolls by and as business challenges worsen, eventually they will wake up to a new shiny technology that "can solve all their problems." The company hastily dashes out and invests millions of dollars on the newest technology only to discover that the "business" does not know how to make it work or why they need to change their

---

[3] Chick-Fil-A Leads Fast Food Industry in Customer Experience According to New Temkim Group Research, http://www.ereleases.com/pr/chickfila-leads-fast-food-industry-customer-experience-temkin-group-research-129258

current practices. Disaster! Too many business leaders go through the motions and really try, but in the end, the efforts fail because they realize after the fact that they did not approach the problem correctly nor did they apply the right level of effort and change to the "business" to support the new technology. These efforts usually end with a very expensive piece of shelfware in the form of technology and a story behind why the business problem still exists (Shelfware: software asset that is paid for but not used and ultimately put on a shelf). The effort is chalked up as a learning experience, and it is back to BAU, or Business as Usual. Business as usual remains the same as it has been for decades—new customer acquisition. Some attention is paid to supporting customers, but the primary focus is all about new acquisition. Does any of this story sound familiar?

Many companies still focus on the acquisition approach to business, constantly building a stream of new customers in which to grow the business. These customer experience "players" are doing something else—*something better*. While they still grow the business through acquisition, they are also investing in their greatest asset—their existing customers. Substantial investments are being made to ensure that their existing customer base not only remains intact, but like a garden, continues to flourish and grow, producing harvest after harvest, year after year.

With competitive forces becoming more imposing by the second and consumers being flooded with choice, many businesses are looking around and starting to wonder where their next profitable customers will come from. Market saturation is no joke! What do you do when penetration rates reach capacity; when everyone knows about your brand and have decided NOT to buy from you? Companies across the globe are realizing that achieving maximum customer value within their existing, deeply penetrated customer base is key to sustainable growth in new sectors. As the marketplace evolves, it will be critical for your business to focus on and leverage your most important asset, current customers.

With new technologies available in the marketplace and a driving business focus centered on the customer, your business can realign its goals to get more value out of your existing customer base. A shift of balance needs to occur within the business from the constant drive for new customer acquisition to focusing on instilling best practices for customer experience and retention.

When this happens, your workforce will focus on outside-of-the-box solutions, including which business capabilities can give you the right information that you need, at the right moment in time, to ensure that customers return to use your products and services again and again, resulting in a continuous revenue stream.

The more your business understands about your customer, the more you will be able to extend the buying pull of your customer and profitability. By aligning your business operations to leverage new technologies and business capabilities, your company will be able to provide the most appropriate interaction for the customer at the right time. This may be as simple as making an offer to your broad subscriber base directly at the moment that they are most likely to buy. This may also be differentiating a customer interaction for that "specific" customer based on segment, past experience, value to the business, or a multitude of other customer insights. The key differentiating factor that will help businesses succeed where others have failed is to "design" consistent and intelligent interactions into your business operations that drive profitability and at the same time leave the customer feeling like you know them personally and CARE about their experience with your brand. Unfortunately, too many businesses are accustomed to the "one-size-fits-all" approach to customer management and are missing out on this valuable opportunity.

Establishing a customer-centric business operation is easier said than done. Now is the time to get on the court and take advantage of new possibilities! In my experience, the possibilities that open up for your business will be vast and life-changing...or at least business culture changing. As you begin to embark on the journey of transforming your business to become customer centric, there will be much temptation to think that you can buy your way to success. Many companies believe that they can purchase technology or software and all of their customer experience issues will vanish. Nothing could be further from the truth! Often companies go out and spend millions to purchase flashy new technology solutions only to have them fail miserably, doing more harm than good to their sales. What is often overlooked is a holistic approach to operationalizing significant change. While purchasing software and or technology may be part of the overall solution to address your business's top challenges, there are other key areas that you will need to contemplate and address along the journey in addition to the technology. Taking action and successfully transforming your business to be more customer-centric using a holistic approach to mitigate risks of failure and driving profitability is what this book is all about. It has been designed to give you the information and approach that you will need to get your company on the "court" and taking action. Throughout the book, we will go through this proven approach in great detail. I call it the TIPP approach to customer experience.

The key advantage the TIPP approach will give you over the competition is that it sets your business up to be successful by overcoming obstacles and expanding customer communications. It allows you to look at the key dimensions that will be needed to create profitable customer interactions and gives you the fortitude and discipline to sustain those interactions over time. It will set your company up to be a "player" on the court of customer experience.

With this new and improved, customer-centric approach to customer experience, data analytics, technology, and business process, your business will be able to practically guarantee that your strategic goals will be realized one interaction at a time, which will directly improve your overall profitability.

Throughout this book, you will learn how to optimize customer interactions to produce the results that you desire for your business. Real time interaction management is about intelligent interactions with your customers that drive loyalty and profitability. It means finding a balance that uses specific interactions to drive dramatic improvements in customer experience while accomplishing strategic goals and ultimately improving the bottom line of your business.

Find out how to take advantage of new technologies, new business theories, and a revolutionary interaction and decision management process to help your company come to terms with this new capability of improving business.

- *Real time interaction management has the potential to open your company up to a whole new method of expansion and optimization.*

By carefully following the advice, lessons learned, and practical steps in this book, your intelligent interactions will eventually become the backbone for your customer-centric approach to sales, retention, and success in the near future. By taking action with this approach and leveraging my firsthand experience and lessons learned, the possibilities and interactions you create will propel your business to new levels of operational efficiency with a customer base that will not only sustain your business but continue to grow it into the future. It is time to play ball!

PART I
Are You Getting the Most Out of Every Customer Interaction?

CHAPTER 1
Defining RTIM as a Business Capability

It is not the strongest of the species that survives, nor the most intelligent, but the one most responsive to change.

CHARLES DARWIN

Every time you sell a product to a customer, answer the phone, or send them marketing content, you are performing a customer interaction. These customer interactions have been used in the past to attract more customers to your business or to sell existing customers more products and services.

As time progresses, so do the needs of your business. Your business capabilities now need to be focused on real time interaction management, namely the operational business decisions made in conjunction with your systems and technologies in order to bring about higher sales and retention rates or lower overall costs to serve.

What Is Real Time Interaction Management?

If you think of a business capability as an expression of the capacity, materials, and expertise that your business needs in order to perform core functions, then real time interaction management is like the symphony conductor that aligns your business functions to create synergy.

A real time interaction manager is a system or program that is used to choose the best way to appeal to a specific customer during an interaction between them and your business. Using intelligent business processes, decision capabilities, and predictive models, additional revenue can be generated as long as customers are exposed to these personalized tactics or messages at the right time in the interaction. With the timing being of the essence, it is critical to link the tactics to consistent business process.

The key to unlocking true customer value lies in understanding how to leverage these decision and process management systems in a way that brings business benefit. This is because at the very heart of all customer interactions is the set of decisions that a person makes in order to close the sale. Which product out of the catalog should you offer this specific customer? Should this customer get a discount? If so, how much should we discount the offer?

What if you could include additional insights into each customer interaction? Such as: What is the value of this customer to my business? Is this customer likely to churn to competition? Should we do something different for this particular customer? How much does this customer cost to serve? Is it worth it?

Building customer value and driving long-term profitability can be linked directly to real time interaction management. It is a way to ensure that your business is not only leveraging the customer analytics data but making the correct decisions based on this data to drive the business processes that get those additional sales and ultimately boost business profitability.

The truth is that we are operating in a fast-paced, real time world that gathers huge volumes of data that few businesses adequately know how to deal with. But what do businesses do with this data? Few businesses have a strategy for how to leverage this data. But I would argue/suggest that data is one of the most important, yet, in parallel, the most under-utilized of resources. Without the right decision management capability in place, much of this crucial data is lost or never used to make a lasting business impact. However, the good news is that it does not have to be this way. With real time interaction management, you can learn how to properly use technology and decision making to increase your business income and add real value to each customer interaction.

Customer Centric Decisioning & Business Process Management

Real time interaction management is made up of two fundamental functions: customer centric analytics and decisioning and business process management. The two different capabilities are fairly simple to define and will help you gain a better understanding of your real time interaction management goals.

Customer centric analytics and decisioning enables your customer centric operating model to deliver consistent messages over multiple channels to every customer in real time—and is therefore a core function or capability needed when implementing a branded customer experience (a customer experience that creates brand personality, i.e., humanizes your brand).

Too many companies still have a prevailing acquisition-based, product-centric culture. They are accustomed to ferociously hunting for more customers—but now they need to switch over to customer loyalty, a completely different business focus. Product proliferation and pushy campaigns have led to customer overload. Customers that are contacted too much switch off.

Inefficient campaigns like this let a lot of money fall through the cracks. Though businesses buy analytics and insight programs to collect valuable data, they are still finding it tough to reach out at the point of interaction on an individual customer basis.

Poor customer experiences are spreading because decisioning for these client-facing activities is fragmented. And this is compounded by rising customer expectations. Customers expect more, and they expect it now. This increased customer pressure is driving the need to rapidly improve customer satisfaction. This is where real time interaction management comes into play. Meeting this customer need and improving satisfaction is ***exactly*** what real time interaction management is designed to do. Moreover, it does so efficiently so that your bottom line is positioned for sustainable growth by reinforcing the base.

Business process management (BPM) aligns an organization's business processes with the wants and needs of their customers. It works in conjunction with technology, integration, innovation, and flexibility to promote efficiency in every process. Simply stated, it is the process of streamlining and optimizing business processes.

Together, you can see how they would work to solve these growing problems—by combining analytical insight with new business strategy to identify optimal customer treatment on a company-wide basis.

Customer centric decisioning and business process management will result in systems that are different from what has come before. They must be agile and able to adapt to changing circumstances so they can be continuously improved. They will be analytical so that you can identify and manage fraud and risk while targeting opportunities based on data analysis.

They will also be adaptive so that your business can find and manage innovative approaches to this new way of doing business.

It is time for your business to get the MOST out of every single customer interaction that takes place across a wide range of channels and media. It will mean evaluating and potentially changing many of your business processes as you adopt customer centric decisioning to streamline and optimize sales opportunities with your existing client base. While this may sound overwhelming, it is absolutely critical.

Who Uses Real Time Interaction Management

As technology has evolved to respond for businesses and the Internet has spread and made it easy for customers and businesses to connect, real time interaction management has grown to become a dominant concern for organizations that are looking for ways to capitalize on their existing customer base.

You would not have to look very far to see the investments that companies are making in their businesses to support this new way of competing. Companies are starting to put their money where their customers are:

- Spending on customer relationship management[4] has boomed according to platforms like Salesforce.com and Microsoft.
- According to Gartner, global spending for all enterprise software is at $304 billion in 2013, with 6.4% growth from 2012.
- Gartner predicts that CRM will grow to be a $36.5 billion market by 2017; that is an annual growth rate of 15.1 percent.

The truth is that all businesses need to effectively manage their inbound and outbound interactions with customers. These interactions happen across many channels, namely mail, email, the web, call centers, and branch offices.

Inbound interactions are an opportunity to connect with the client based on their needs. They will visit your website or make a call because at that specific time, they need something from you— be it information or assistance. Outbound interactions are used to target products within specific customer segments based on analytics data.

These interactions can be very successful, but it depends on

---

[4] Jennifer LeClaire, CRM Booming, Business Process management Critical Too, http://www.cio-today.com/story.xhtml?story_id=1030063W5ROV&page=1&full_skip=1

the business's understanding of their customer's needs and wants at the time. To get a real time view of each customer is highly valuable, as it streamlines the decision making process once these interactions are taking place.

Organizations of every size create, build, or purchase information systems. They use these systems to house their important information on products, services, customers, suppliers, and more. Everyone in the organization uses these information systems. The problem is that these systems tend to wait rather than act. They escalate instead of empower; they report, but they do not learn. No real change takes place.

Many businesses are already using real time interaction management systems. According to Netpromoter.com,[5] 8 out of 10 U.S. banks and 8 out of the 10 top telecommunications companies in the world use these new information systems. Not to mention corporate giants like American Express, Apple, eBay, PayPal, and Charles Schwab that also have the highest net promoter score in the industry.

A need arises to develop something like a real time interaction management system to control and adapt these unchangeable processes. More and more businesses across the globe are realizing that real time interaction management is where they will get the most profit for their customer interactions.

Everyone from medium-sized organizations to Fortune 100 companies is integrating real time interaction management systems into their businesses. They are doing it to improve customer centric decisioning and business processes discussed earlier. They are shifting their focus to take advantage of their existing customer base instead of purely focusing on the older model of new client acquisition.

We are living in a boom period, where executives that want to find new ways of increasing profitability are exploring these real time systems. They understand that in today's environment, the

---

[5] Net Promoter Benchmarking, http://www.netpromoter.com/why-net-promoter/compare/

secret to tomorrow's dollars lies in the most precious asset they have—their existing customer base.

They understand that an agile, analytic, and adaptive framework needs to be established in order to do this. Many companies that have already spent time implementing real time interaction management into their business are benefitting from it already; however, not all businesses are successful the first, second, or third time. Adopting a proven approach to tackling this new way of business will prove to be critical in the months and years to come.

These are the companies that will manage to hold onto their customer bases, even in the face of new technology, new services, and greater competition. In this way, real time interaction management also acts as a protective model to ensure the continued improvement of your company, even when new customers are not being actively acquired.

Proof That It Works

Where is the proof that real time interaction management is actually a better model than the past customer acquisition focus? Businesses all over the world are discovering how much of an impact a quality process and decision management system can have on their companies. With the rising customer demand and the limited functionality of data systems, a solution like this is really the only viable option when you are looking for agile, analytic, and adaptive systems that take action.

Take a beauty retailer for example. It sells beauty products to millions of customers spread over 1,500 locations worldwide. Every year there are tens of millions of transactions because of its loyalty program. There is a constant series of promotions, two rounds every month, with each round comprising 50 items.

There are also discounts on combinations of products bought at the same time, local promotions, and other running specials. This took ages for its IT department, and the rollout format was very restricted. Front-end sellers would get very confused about the constant promotions, and not all customers would get their complete rewards.

The beauty retailer therefore developed a real time interaction management system to take care of these promotions and programs. The system used point-of-sales transactions, customer profiles, sales history, and other data to ensure that all applicable customer discounts and loyalty rewards were automatically calculated.

The system itself made the pricing decision for the retailer. That decision resulted in a guarantee that all great customers would get the greatest discount and would spend even more money on beauty products, as the marketing promotions and materials worked like a charm just as they were designed to. This is just one example of how adequate decision management and correct interactions can lead to increases in sales for a global company.

Overall, you are looking at improvements for changing circumstances, process improvements, and compliance in an agile system. Your analytics system will help identify risk, reduce fraud, and focus resources and will assist with targeting and retaining customers. Finally, with an adaptive system, you will find new approaches as you are able to test and learn. This, in turn, will help you manage trade-offs, and continuous improvement will result.

The real proof that real time interaction management works comes down to numbers. The difference between good companies and great companies is usually incorporating small changes that address big opportunities. When you have huge volumes of transactions, and you create a system that makes it easy to measure the efficiency of a new system like this, you will see the benefit and learn to predict the future of your business. Across the board, it seems that wherever real time interaction management systems are being placed with the focus on aligning these systems to business benefit, rapid improvements result.

This means that profits increase, customer loyalty improves, and marketing or sales promotions become far more effective as the timing and method of delivery is correct. If you can harness the power of a system like this, you will be able to increase the profitability of your business while guaranteeing that you are getting the most out of each customer interaction.

Interactions, Scale, and Expectations

With changing expectations and scale, it is nearly impossible for businesses to adequately meet the needs of their customers, employees, suppliers, and partners. Interactions within an organization change when these other elements adapt. Consumers are now mobile and social—which has significantly changed how you do business.

The Internet has also massively affected the way you do business and interact with your customers. New interactions must evolve from a new information system. Mobile interactions are very important right now, as this is where many of your customers are interacting. Things have recently moved from PC to mobile, which means your interactions must change.

Social interactions have also been rapidly evolving since the rise of social media. Customers are reviewing and chatting about brands all the time now. How do you leverage that? New data needs to be pulled from these channels, analyzed, and integrated into your real time interaction management system.

Distributed interactions on the web have resulted in a huge amount of shopping options for customers. Customers once bought from their nearest shop; now they buy from a platform that has the best deal. There is far more price-checking before buying, and the focus is now on value. Simply having the cheapest product is not working anymore; now you need to have the cheapest and highest value product on offer. Every customer defines value differently; that is where these personalized interactions come in handy.

Scale is also changing in business, which further aggravates the problem. Data explosions because of the web, social media, and data mining result in high volume analytics. Big data means that every single transaction is being recorded and every conversation about a product is being tracked on social media sites. Audio, video, image, and copy content are out there.

Information systems need to be used to store and manage this influx of information. The pressure has increased to become more efficient. More must be done with less, meaning that business operations must be supported by small cost increases. The same number of people need to do more work. These information systems need to be smarter to help them handle the work.

Eventually, businesses will need to adopt systems that require few human interactions to process transactions. These transaction volumes will grow, and more products mean more customers, sales, and employees. Everything about transactions must be automatically managed on an efficient scale.

When costs rise and your analysis shows you must outsource your core system work to affordable providers, how do you deliver a consistent customer experience that still drives your brand when you use outsourcing? With the right planning, you can align your outsourcing work with your customer experience strategy. It is a great way to drive your strategy forward while diluting the cost burden of the full-time equivalent.

This all culminates in changing expectations. Consumer expectations are now all about real time, "instant" responses. The need arises to secure systems that can do this for them. Real time responsiveness is paramount. Do you remember the old days of going to the bank, filling in paper forms, and waiting in queues? Now it is a one-click solution.

Real time responsiveness will be a challenge to get right, but it is all tied up with the systems they are using. People cannot achieve this; only their systems can. Global customers expect global service, which means brand-wide consistency at multiple locations. Again, the only thing that can achieve such an ideal is an intelligent system.

People want self service so that they can directly interact with your brand when they need to. Information systems that allow a high level of personalized self service must be implemented. We live in a 24/7 world that never sleeps. Clearly, the onus is on these modern information systems to reach the level of service that customers expect from businesses. They expect real time interaction management systems, and your brand is responsible for making them happen.

What Does RTIM Mean for Your Business?

In the old days, enterprise-centric sales ran the roost. Businesses only cared about the number and amount of products being sold because that is how you would make the most money. Only now, with all these new demands and technological advancements, this is not how you make the most money anymore. People are where the money lies.

Since the advent of social media and the rise of the Internet, a new power has surfaced. Predictive analytics has shown all of us that people-centric data can be used to capitalize on individuals. More sales can result when you know the right time, the right medium, and the right message and/or tactic to use.

Decision management systems can now be powered by predictive analytics to make the dream of mass customization a reality. This is the new market we all face as business owners and global brands.

Customers demand intimacy, and it is impossible to solely rely on automated systems that treat everybody the same. Automated systems can and will alienate people from your company. Without leveraging intelligent insights to drive interactions, automated systems risk driving more customer frustration than they do driving company benefit. It excludes your customers from having a good experience by standardizing the communication process for the "average" customer, rendering it impersonal and difficult to use. There is no such thing as an "average" customer in today's marketplace.

Instead, using operational excellence and product leadership, we can combine decision-making systems with predictive analytic systems to form the basis for a successful real time interaction management system that will excel at these new demands on modern business.

You will find as an executive or company CEO that your organization desperately needs to discover a way to intimately reach each and every customer. Securing customer reach involves making the "product" or "service" promise (product leadership), keeping the promise (customer intimacy), and delivering the promise (operational excellence). They all work together to deliver on these new global expectations to produce a decision management system that consists of recommendation engines, systems, and treatment engines.[6]

Effective personalization requires the anticipation of a customer need. These needs can be identified if there is an ongoing "conversation" or connection between the brand and the customer. Your customers want service providers they can access anywhere at any time.

Fraud and tax evasion are taken into account with new information systems. In order to keep these systems crime-free, rule changes can occur in real time so that patterns of illicit behavior are easier to spot. A good decision management system can also maximize your assets, but mostly it maximizes your revenue and profit.

Dynamic pricing can now be a reality with the speed of these new systems, as can decisions based on price determination and long- and short-term demands in an ever-changing market. You will be able to negotiate better supplier deals, reduce deal conflicts, and provide sales targets for your merchandisers as the market fluctuates.

On the whole, real time interaction management systems are far more agile, analytic, and adaptive than the traditional information systems that you are currently using. They move and evolve with the market and work for the benefit of your customer. This results in a total business process revamp and improvements in many core areas.

---

[6] James Taylor, The Decision Management Manifesto Explained, http://www.slideshare.net/jamet123

What most enterprise centric businesses do not understand is that their competition has already figured out this fundamental truth and is taking real steps to guarantee that in the future, their existing customer base will provide them with the income they need to grow.

CHAPTER 2

Why Do You Need Real Time Interaction Management?

> *"Any fool can make things bigger, more complex, and more violent. It takes a touch of genius—and a lot of courage—to move in the opposite direction."*
>
> ALBERT EINSTEIN

Real time interaction management has been brought to your attention out of a real need to replace out-dated systems with systems that work. Most of all, there is a need to replace fixed systems with those that are changeable so that they can adapt and evolve along with your business in the coming years.

There are pressing reasons why you need real time interaction management, and this chapter is about explaining those reasons. Initially, let's begin with the core problem—the old systems—and work our way out from there.

The "Burning Platform"

Traditionally in business, a burning platform is a term used to describe an extremely compelling business situation in order to convey—in the most serious method possible—*the immediate need for change.*

The "burning platform"[7] story goes something like this: One night back in 1988, an oil platform off the coast of Scotland exploded into flames. One of the sixty-three crew members who survived was Andy Mochan, a superintendent on the rig.

From the hospital, he told of being awakened by the explosion and alarms. Badly injured, he escaped from his quarters to the platform edge. Beneath him, oil had surfaced and ignited. Twisted steel and other debris littered the surface of the water. Because of the water's temperature, he knew that he could live a maximum of only twenty minutes if not rescued. Despite all that, Andy jumped fifteen stories from the platform to the water.

When asked why he took that potentially fatal leap, he did not hesitate. He said, "It was either jump or fry." He chose possible death over certain death. Andy jumped because he felt he had no choice—the price of staying on the platform was too high.

Using the burning platform story, you can call attention to a commitment issue in business relatively quickly. On my first encounter with this principle, it brought to mind the images of the burning oil rig that has been set on fire. This platform is usually where you would stand to perform your daily work. The only problem, of course, is that the edges are on fire, and soon you will run out of platform and be consumed in the flames.

It is really a warning for all businesses following the old enterprise-centric method of selling. Eventually, the whole world is going to know about your brand, and the choice will be made by every individual—whether they like you or dislike you.

The flames surrounding this burning platform indicate that you have a limited amount of time to implement these new changes. You can either jump into the freezing water below and take a shot at a new way of survival, or you can stay on your platform and know that you will be destined to experience imminent death. Driving real time interaction management across your organization is like

---

[7] http://www.connerpartners.com/frameworks-and-processes/the-real-story-of-the-burning-platform

jumping into the freezing water. When you look around at what other businesses are doing in this new business climate, you will start to realize that many have already made the plunge to the freezing water. Will it be painful if you jump? Possibly. Will you survive and eventually be much better off than where you started? More likely. The point is real time interaction management is going to become business as usual across the globe, so the earlier you make the plunge to accept the possibility of a new way of business, the better.

The burning platform analogy used in this context tells you that soon you will not have any choice at all. Customer-centric decisioning and business process management are must haves in the up and coming loyalty wars.

The brands that excel will be the ones that embrace the use of technology and customer-centric strategy to sell their products and services to their existing customer base. While they are doing this, other companies will be forced to downsize, retrench, or worse—because sheer economics will tell you that yesterday's approach to business is not sustainable in today's competitive environment. As the supply of "good" customers dries up, the demand for those customers rise; as a result, associated acquisition costs will rise and, over time, eat away profits. Eventually, they are unable to find and convert new people into profitable customers. Game over.

This is perhaps the most pressing reason of all—to change over now. You are on a burning platform, and time is running out. Real time interaction management can save you and your company from the ever-increasing demands of the instant consumer culture, but your business will have to make the jump.

The Product & Service Centric Business vs. The Customer Centric Business

Do you remember the mantra—the customer is king? It is still being used today, even though it first came to light in the early

'80s. The truth, of course, is that companies have been very one sided when it comes to their customer base and not as "customer oriented" as the slogan would have you believe.

However, this was perhaps the first instance where the enterprise took notice of the "customer" as an important part of sales. These days we know that with enough data and strategy, any customer can be prompted to buy again and again—gaining your organization that repeat business that you so desperately need for top sales.

We are living in a transition period—the product and service centric business is going up against the newly formed customer centric business. New technology has presented thousands of options to customers, and they are pickier than ever before.

Instead, businesses are waking up to the fact that they can earn a lot more income from their existing client bases. Once you have a customer that uses your services, it is just a matter of getting to know them better before you can begin to suggest products and services that they will genuinely want.

As you can tell, a customer centric business puts the customer first—they are the focus of predictive analytics, and they are the reason that decision management systems need to be so streamlined. For the first time, I would say that the customer is finally king in this new model.

Product and service based businesses are going to struggle to find new markets to break into now that information moves so fast. As competition rises and markets shrink, you will need to find a way to continue to expand and bring in new sources of revenue.

The obvious choice is to implement new information systems to help you optimize the sales processes with the customers that already support your brand. You cannot really compare the two anymore—one has fast become a burning platform, and the other is a progressive new mode of doing business that is adaptable, flexible, and desirable to the modern customer.

It has been proven that a multitude of choices leads to alienation. Customers have literally become paralyzed with the paradox of choice thanks to the Internet and ever-increasing speeds of information dissemination.

The big difference between product and service based businesses and customer centric businesses is that the former continues to offer range and choice, which results in less sales because of this paralysis. Customer centric businesses, on the other hand, do not require people to work to make decisions or choices. Interactions should not feel like "work" to the customer.

They are given simple, basic options based on what they like—and they are given the opportunity to buy it from a brand they trust. This always results in more sales because of the reduction of choice.

Your customers will also appreciate the simplicity of choice, as real time interaction management is reflective of the specific customer during the interaction. This means that choices will become more exact, as they are based on proven statistics and probability. The "most likely" decision will always be suggested to drive processes that suit the customer's needs. Choices made by businesses that are product centric feel like work to customers because they do not contemplate the specific needs of the customer. Real time interaction management in contrast is a vacation for the customer in that it comparatively reflects the choices of specific customers in each interaction made.

The Culture of Customer Loyalty

Your business culture needs to transcend country-specific culture. You need a way to reach people all over the world and make them listen to you. They need to like you, trust you, and be willing to keep in semi-permanent contact with you.

A global business culture is key to re-aligning your external customer experience structure. If you are going to reach and retain customers in multiple countries—securing their loyalty beyond borders—you will need to work on "globalizing" the overall customer experience in your company.

Southwest Airlines[8] has had enormous success with intelligent interactions. Their sales teams were selling less, so they refocused on customer retention, upselling and cross selling, the lifetime value of a customer, and overall revenue from their existing customer base.

Service became their major differentiator, and they launched new predictive analytics and decision management systems to help them get there. They improved the customer experience with multi-channel support, they reduced customer effort and frustration, and they increased customer loyalty.

The very simple formula was better service and less frustration. And this is really the real time interaction management method. Make it easy for your existing clients to buy repeatedly from you because you are the best, and they will do it. Once you have a customer in your sales cycle, it is up to you to identify opportunities, target them, provide better experiences, and get more sales in a non-intrusive manner.

That is essentially the culture of customer loyalty. Customers are loyal to brands that provide an excellent quality of service and that resolve faults, frustrations, and issues very quickly. It all depends on your information systems and how effective your decision management system is when working in conjunction with predictive analytics.

Whereas customer loyalty was once viewed as a department in a business, now it needs to be viewed as the business itself. We can agree that customer loyalty needs to be viewed on a holistic basis. It has got to be enterprise wide if real change is going to happen.

Types of Loyalty / Retention

- *Reactive* – Trying to be loyal or "save the customer" once the customer has expressed an interest in leaving you

---

8   Parature, http://www.slideshare.net/parature/how-southwest-airlines-built-a-culture-of-customer-loyalty

- ***Proactive*** – Refining tactics to proactively create loyalty when you believe the customer *may* want to leave you (many service calls, mediocre survey responses, etc.)
- ***Preemptive*** – Targeting the customer and instilling loyalty/retention *before they even know* they might want to leave you

Real time interaction management reshapes your business to become a fully customer centric enterprise, where loyalty is not just a passing thought but a very serious core function. It is the exact methods that will help your business continue to be financially successful for many years into the future.

Right now, your customer loyalty may be a program or a series of programs that is handled by a specific department. But this is part of enterprise centric sales. You need to shift over to customer centric sales, which means that customer loyalty has to be integrated into your business culture and across business functions.

This can only be done with real time interaction management; namely business process and decision management systems fueled by predictive analytics. You are living in a time when the customer has all the power. The only way to reclaim some of this power for your brand is to treat them like they really matter—and they do. They are your sales. They are your business.

Functional Silos and the Ideal Customer Experience

In business, a functional silo is usually a stand-alone business function that works in conjunction with other business functions. As a single silo, they are considered to be dysfunctional and less communicative and collaborative when compared with the improved cross-functional organizations available today.

The real problem is that these functional silos have been around for decades, "helping" businesses manage their workload and adding something to the overall customer experience.

Unfortunately, this customer experience strategy is almost always horrible.

Take your average corporate call center for example. A customer begins to experience faults with their service. They call the center for assistance. First, they are rerouted to a second phone number, so they have to call again. An automated *Interactive Voice Response* (IVR) assistant lists a number of departments they can contact. They select a number and have to wait for one to ten minutes—while listening to bad music—for an agent to answer.

Finally, an agent answers and they give their name, phone number, address, and client details to this person. A few seconds later they are told they "are not with the right group" and to hold for the next person that can help them. They are transferred multiple times to multiple departments, and each time they are forced to give their details again.

Has this ever happened to you? What emotions did this experience evoke for you? Does this sound like an acceptable customer experience in today's marketplace? Often this experience is really driven from a company's internal functional silos "baggage," which usually equates to more work and frustration for the customer. Who needs another job?

The business may believe that this works, but in the context of customer experience, it is about the worst standing silo there is. After being on hold for 30 minutes and having to explain the issue multiple times to many different people, the customer is finally helped. Even though there was a successful outcome, the customer experience was damaged.

Every time the customer experience is damaged, loyalty drops. Your risk of losing that customer increases. This customer will listen the next time one of your competitors promotes their services. They already know that your service is dreadful. And at some point, the grass starts looking greener with your competitor. These functional silos play their part in business, but they need to be aligned to effectively impact the customer experience in a positive way.

Imagine this same experience—only designed to be customer centric. The customer calls in and is instantly directed to an agent (who is best matched by skill level to service them and their type of segment), who takes their details once. They are put on hold for a short time to execute processes specific to their needs, enough time to run some personalized upsell voice communications through the on hold IVR system. The next person has all their details in front of them. They provide excellent quality service specific to the customer's needs.

In less than half of the time the problem is solved because of the much more intelligent and efficient system. You just helped the customer, and you also helped the company by effectively reducing the cost to serve. The customer is completely satisfied and may even buy that new service you told them about when they were on hold. The customer is happy, and you have made a new sale. This is essentially what real time interaction management can do for you—it breaks down the walls of functional silos and drives a customer-centric experience that also drives strategic benefits to your business.

Customer Contact Management

Does your business have a holistic strategy on how and when they touch the customer? Or is it pretty much anytime a specific business function wants to? There is another core reason why you need real time interaction management in your business right now. It is called customer contact management—and it is a division of customer relationship management.

How do you currently connect and maintain contact with existing and prospective customers? My hunch is that it is part of your customer relationship strategy, but you have never clearly outlined your contact framework. Many businesses share this problem. They do the bare minimum, or they move forward without an enterprise-wide contact strategy and abuse their customer base by over-contacting them.

A great customer contact management framework will have you analyzing current practices and highlighting areas for improvement. Yes, this is a form of relationship stimulation, but it is called "contact" management because the response that you get from your customers is greatly reliant on the way you reach out to them in the first place.

To adequately execute a customer contact management strategy, you will need an adaptable system that is fueled by high quality customer data that is collected from multiple channels. A distinction must be made between leads (new customers) and records (existing customers)—as you will be focusing on records for best results.

With the right tools and technology, you can scale the intensity of the customer contact as the system allows for a far more intimate level of message customization and personalization. Once this is done, you will look at the outputs of your customer contact management activities, or the results.

You will then use these results to make some challenging decisions based on individual customers, segments, or groups. When you properly manage the way you contact your customers, you are in a better position to communicate effectively with them. That means that they will enjoy a more personal experience from you, at the right time, through the right communication channel that they prefer.

This sits at the core of all customer relationship strategies, which fall under the new progressive methods used in intelligent business interactions. By reaching out to your customers and making them feel unique, special, and well looked after, you can cause repeat sales from a single individual, which will increase your annual profit margins one interaction at a time.

Real time interaction management goes a long way to producing enough know-how for this level of customer-centric contact to happen. When you can make decisions about a customer based on past interactions and future sales, your perspective changes.

The customer will be contacted using the correct contact channels, tactics, inputs, outputs, and tools that will fuel the right kind of business between brands and their customers. Customer dialogue, relationship management, partner services, data management, channel customization, brand community, and customer benefits will all be enhanced with this new method of client contact.

Analytics and Insight for Business Management

With the rise of new customer touchpoints such as the Internet and social media platforms, data from the contact channels in which your customer engages you has become the most invaluable tool for customer-centric businesses. There has been a steep evolution toward fact-based decision making across many different niches. We see it in the medical field with evidence-based medicine and in the business field with real time interaction management.

Running a successful business in this global market is fiercely competitive, and it requires more than simply "business smarts" or "guesswork" to get it right. The average business needs to have an edge so that they can survive and thrive. I like to call this edge getting to know your customer base.

Finding patterns of performance and new ways to reduce inefficiencies is all part of the wonderful world of measuring analytics. When you focus on predictive analytics, you can make better, faster decisions that are much more likely to work for your business.

Business analytics is the practice of collecting and using data to drive business strategy and performance. It has not only been proven to work but it can shatter any previous methods of improving revenue by a significant margin. This is because all decisions are based on qualified data that tell you something important about your operations and the customer.

Analytics and insights are indispensible for good business management these days. The next step on this hierarchy is to target individual customers so that you can service them individually in unique ways that serve their needs and improve customer loyalty.

It is impossible to do this without the right technology and business analytics systems. The demand for company performance is growing, and this is one of the frontiers that have yet to be broached by many executives in large companies. While they may use analytics in their business intelligence reporting, it has yet to become common for driving interactions with individual customers.

Business management is about collecting the industry knowledge, functional capabilities, and technical sophistication that will lead your company toward high conversions on a per customer basis. This is real time interaction management as it is presented on a large scale.

While the task seems monumental with many businesses having millions of individual clients, technology and accurate decisioning models make it possible. When you gain more business insights, your decision making improves. Applying this to your new customer-centric ideology will do incredible things for your business:

- Convert individual customers more often, increasing sales-per-customer, which improves profits
- Increase viral sharing potential as streamlined messages cause higher engagement rates, which improves online SEO and sales
- Gain valuable insights on what your actual customers want for better product research and development in future

These are just some of the far reaching effects of RTIM.

Analytics and insights for business management will also help your company manage their risks in a more productive manner. With less risk, reduced customer complaints, and increased levels of service, you are bound to make a real impact with this new application for business analytics systems.

Cross-Functional Interactions and the 5Ps of strategy

A major reason to use real time interaction management systems is because of the cross functional interactions that will either gradually improve sales and customer relationships or be a frustration point for the customer. Even though different people within your organization will interact with different customers during your average day, you need their front line decisions and goals to be consistent and aligned with your strategy.

Cross-functional interactions involve a number of people within your workforce working together towards a common goal; in this case, improved customer retention and sales. It does not matter if someone from the service department or the sales department is talking to your customer; the interactions will be consistent because they will result from the same foundation of data, insights, processes, and decisioning models.

This will help your company achieve higher levels of consistency, responsiveness, innovation, and efficiency. When everyone in your business knows what their ultimate purpose is, it does not take long before everyone is working to proliferate this goal.

In 1987 Henry Mintzberg wrote about the 5Ps of strategy. They are plan, ploy, pattern, position, and perspective. To take full advantage of your businesses strengths and capabilities, you need to use each one of these 5Ps in your cross functional interactions.

Cross-functional interactions should take advantage of this strategy methodology to help individuals within your company align their communication to achieve the desired result. Cross-functional interactions need to be planned—how will they be best delivered to the customer to suit your goals?

There needs to be ploys—how is your interaction going to disrupt the strategy of your competitors the best? Then you need to establish patterns based on past organizational behavior and collected in your information systems. Everyone within your organization needs to have access to this information so that they are informed and can present a unified company experience to the customer.

Cross-functional interactions are also about your position in the marketplace. As we discussed earlier, it is the new "marketplace of one," so your business needs to figure out how to treat people like individuals across all departments and divisions. There needs to be a consistency in the treatment of your customers.

Finally, for cross-functional interactions to be successful, you need to integrate a customer-centric culture into your company, essentially changing your perspective on the way you do business. This process will result in the correct implementation and dissemination of real time interaction management systems company wide.

The 5Ps are just a simple way of showing you how powerful your interactions can be if you take the time to adequately integrate real time interaction management into your new business culture. Think of it as a tool in your tool belt as you begin to define and link strategy to interactions. Everyone will benefit—your sales and support teams, your managers, and your customers most of all.

The Rise of Customer Expectations

Customers want it now. They want it right now. You will never know when that "now" will come, but for 95% of businesses in the world today, "now" is a long way away. New technology has resulted in a spoiled consumer public that demands the best possible service from all brands, all the time. Their expectations are currently disproportionate to the service they are getting.

Today, you can get information instantly, and that is as fast as it gets. It is the reason why it is called "real time" because the moment the customer decides to ask the question, they have the answer. It all hinges on this new culture of information.

Because the Internet has made communication possible, fast, and easy for everyone, brands cannot hide behind their iron thrones anymore. The moment you mess up a disgruntled customer will tell the world about it on Facebook. Today, you lose customers in real time.

So it is not only important to rise to meet these demanding expectations, but it is crucial for the sustainability of your customer-centric business model. Aside from price, customers demand speed, diversity, customization, and top-notch service. They can afford to be picky about the brands they choose to use.

We have a customer-controlled economy where demands must be met. The only way to accurately do this is to predict their needs and manage their expectations. What does this better than real time interaction management? Nothing! It is the reason why it is replacing the old ways of doing business and is revolutionizing the way you will do business in the future.

If you can effectively reduce customer stress, hassle, and concern while simultaneously meeting their every need instantly, easily, and professionally, there is a place for your brand in the future. Online shopping has made customers less aware of where they buy and more aware of what they are buying.

That is why if you can suggest the right products to your individual customer base at the right time, you can take advantage of a large, untapped source of revenue for your company. Customers will continue to reward brands that bother to take the time to get to know them. The brands that treat them the best and provide value will always have their business.

This is why real time interactions management is so crucial in business today. In a short time, perhaps only months from now, your business will realize that customer expectations have ruined all of your existing sales strategies. Sales will diminish, and you will be forced to pick up the pieces of your business.

If, however, you focus on a customer-centric business model right now and learn to effectively manage client expectations, your business will excel in the future. That is not a prediction; it is happening already. You have noticed that change needs to happen;

it is why you are taking the time to read this book! So now let's talk about *how* we make this transformation happen for *your* business!

PART II
Readiness and Preparation: Using the TIPP Approach

CHAPTER 3
Strategy and Technology Readiness and Preparation

"You'll never have a product or price advantage again. They can be easily duplicated, but a strong customer service culture can't be copied."

JERRY FRITZ

It is important that your organization fully understands how to initiate real time interaction management on an enterprise scale, and this means going through the readiness and preparation stages of initiation.

I have created an approach that you can use that will help you understand each aspect of the real time interaction management transformation process so that you will be able to properly introduce, design, deploy, and sustain RTIM in a way that drives profitability for your company.

One thing to note is that this approach focuses on the business operations side of Real Time Interaction Management. While technology is contemplated, TIPP is not a technology-focused approach. Technology is merely one "lens" that you will look through in your journey. Instead, this holistic approach is a way to ensure that the RTIM capabilities your business invests in can be used to drive increased profit to your bottom line while enhancing the customer experience along the way.

The TIPP Approach: Transforming Your Organization

The TIPP approach to real time interaction management focuses on the central elements or dimensions that are concerned with intelligent interactions for your business. If you are going to transform your organization, you will need to know how each dimension plays its part in making the overall system function as a singular unit.

The TIPP approach is comprised of the following dimensions, and the acronym stands for the following:

- **T**echnology and strategy linkage (data, integration, and methods)
- **I**ntelligence (customer and operational insights)
- **P**rocess (how the business people perform their functions)
- **P**eople (the human and non-human elements of each interaction)

When you start to look at the interaction you want to design, you start the TIPP approach "backwards." So first you think about the interaction from a SPPIT perspective, and when you then begin to build the interaction, you reverse engineer the process.

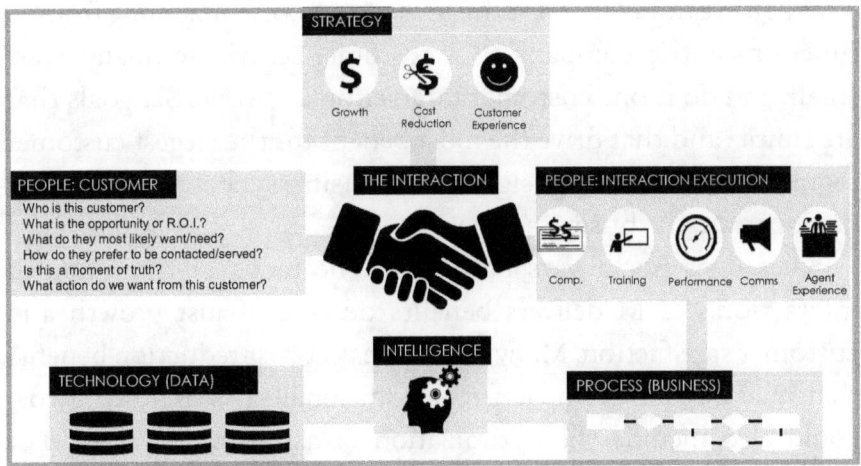

TIPP Approach: A human contact channel example

- In order to provide the right kind of interaction, your business will begin at technology or data gathered.
- The intelligence produced by the targeted, gathered data will help you establish better business processes.
- Once your processes are established, your people can take over implementing, perfecting, testing, and guaranteeing good interactions and engagement.
- Based on their interactions, you can gather MORE data and find out more about each customer.
- This will help you build a solid strategy based on growth, cost reductions, and customer satisfaction.

If you are able to successfully leverage the TIPP approach, you can expect your real time interaction management systems to have holistic change management visibility and work smoothly and efficiently across multiple business functions and contact channels. Initially, the transformation will result in several benefits for your company that will grow over time as you learn and evolve each interaction. These benefits will be the driving factors that influence cultural change.

When you begin to transform your organization from a function-centric company to a customer-centric company, start small, and do it one customer interaction at a time. Set goals that are simple and that drive the most benefit for the largest customer segment while solving significant business challenges as you demonstrate the business benefits

Sales does not always have to be the focus of the intended interaction. RTIM delivers benefits outside of just growth and customer satisfaction. Many companies get cost reduction benefits that may be just as impactful as additional sales. Reducing cost could also include the optimization of assets and revenue. For example, in information-centric industries, real time interaction management can be an effective tool in maximizing the value of your company assets. The Ohio State Office of Budget and Management,[9] for example, implemented business process management software to improve time-to-value and reduce internal capital expenses and overheads.

Previously, they were hampered by manually-driven, outdated processes. Once BPM was established, they managed to coordinate the work of teams across departments and systems and improve their inventory systems and overall budgets—saving them millions of dollars in recurring savings.

A call center can use this data and decisioning process to optimize their energy and network usage—resulting in better infrastructure and reduced costs overall. Transforming your business is not going to be easy, but it is necessary. The good news is that with greater information come improved services across the board.

---

9 State of Ohio Office of Budget and Management, Appian, http://www.appian.com/bpm-customers/story/state-of-ohio-obm.jsp

How Strategy Readiness and Preparation Equate to Results

Where is the value in preparing for this new real time interaction management strategy before acting on it? The value lies in the end results. When you take the time to fully understand the technology, strategy, and data that you will be using to base your decisions on, it will lead to better choices at the end stage—when customers decide to take the actions you anticipate.

As you probably already know, these systems are not insignificant investments for companies. We are usually talking millions just in technology costs. Having done multiple implementations, I can tell you the fastest way to waste this investment is to not be thinking about how it will enable your strategies and drive Return on Investment to your business long term. Linking strategic objectives to interaction performance is critical and, I would say, the first step in preparing your journey with RTIM. Many resource cycles will be avoided, and a better business outcome will result when you define what success looks like before you even consider buying a single piece of technology. It should be the first step you perform.

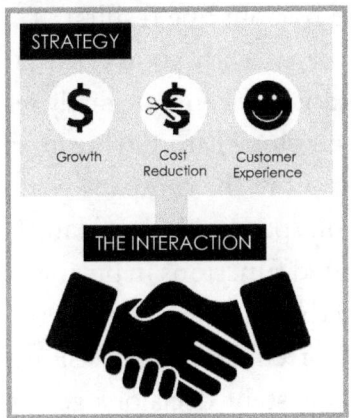

TIPP Approach: Linking strategy to the Interaction

Strategy drivers are:

- Growth: Trying to make the business grow
- Cost reductions: Trying to reduce overall cost to serve
- Customer satisfaction: Trying to increase customer satisfaction with your brand

The interesting thing about this capability is that you actually have the capability to accomplish single or multiple strategies at the same time. Many times people will think these platforms are single threaded and serve only one business function. Make sure stakeholders are never under the impression that RTIM is communicated as "selling" tools, or "troubleshooting process," or "fraud detection" tools when in fact they are actually capable of driving multiple distinct strategies with every interaction. Because of the power in this capability, I would advise you to start small and be deliberate when you tackle your first interaction.

Real time interaction management is not a "tool" for business or a piece of a new technology. It is a fundamental business capability that integrates dynamic, intelligent, and flexible solutions into your company, which results in increased profit generation. Businesses do not need extra tools or "things" to improve their business; they need new business capabilities that drive bottom line results!

In other words, it matters that you begin with your eventual decisions or interactions in mind. Information systems are rarely set up and left to run. They are continuously developed around business data, functions, and processes that will improve the company goal.

If a system is data centric, it will focus on specific kinds of data. If a system is functional, it will support related functions in business, like IT or human resources. It is assumed that people will make the decisions in these evolving systems. They often do make decisions, but unfortunately, they are not often consistent decisions across humans or interactions. That is outdated, and it does not work consistently. Instead, you need decision management systems that put the intended, most profitable decision in mind first.

With this approach, all systems are built with the best final decision in mind. Automation and improvement become common throughout the process. It is not only people that make the decisions but the technology that is chosen to assist in the automation process that becomes the guide for the user.

Strategy readiness and preparation is concerned with the specific decisions that you will make during the design and implementation of your real time interaction management systems. These decisions need to be understood so that you can put together the best kind of system for your business. If you can define a decision-making approach to a system because it is repeated often, this is a great candidate for a decision management system.

- *Strategic decisions*: These guide the direction of your company; they are high value, and there are not many of them. One-off decisions by senior management are a good example of these types of decisions. Lots of information is processed and many options considered. These decisions need to be made by people, not decision management systems.
- *Operational decisions*: These are usually of low individual value and relate to a specific customer or one transaction. They are very important to the overall operation of the system but do not greatly affect the business. Consistency and repeatability are crucial in operational decision making.
- *Tactical decisions*: Control and management concerns are focused tactical decisions. They are of medium value but can still have a big impact on the business. Data and analysis is common by people in charge. Many of these decisions are repeatable and can be handled by decision management systems.

Understanding these key decision areas are the initial strategy that you need to consider when preparing for real time interaction management systems. Knowing where to apply the correct interaction and decision management system will always equate to bottom line results for your business.

How to Assess Current Business Capabilities

How do you assess the current capabilities of your business? Information systems that are used in business today are usually hard coded and very difficult and expensive to change. Programming language tells them what to do, and they do it. When you want to change code, it becomes a costly challenge. This is because you have to confirm that the changes to your code are doing what they were meant to do and explain it to the business in a way that they decide to invest the capital dollars needed to make the adjustments.

Information technology projects have to be budgeted, planned, and executed well in advance in order to make changes to an existing system. This is a very costly approach in the long run and has a huge negative impact to the speed in which you can get these changes to market. This is where your current system probably stands, with dozens of segregated systems that are fixed and nearly impossible to change.

When you implement your decision management systems, this cannot happen. You have to replace opacity with transparency. These modern systems are expected to comply with regulations and company policies. In other words, you have to be able to see HOW a decision was made and an interaction performed.

If experts in the field barely understand the old code, then it is likely that the code is incorrect or outdated. Your first step will be to have your existing systems checked for these fixed, redundant concerns. When regulations change, so must the behavior of any decent process or decision management system.

These processes and decisions will be based on the new policies and regulations of the business so that correct or effective decisions are constantly made in the right places. Decisions made on the expectations of customers have to be competitive, but because customer behavior changes all the time, your process and decision management system must change as well.

The new design of your real time interaction management system must be transparent so that it is obvious to everyone that it is performing the right functions and behaviors at all times. This transparency will show the user how the decision was made so that it spreads system understanding.

The system itself must also be flexible so that it can change with the needs and demands of an ever-changing consumer public as well as your shifting business priorities and objectives. Design transparency is one of these key elements that is most likely missing in your current system infrastructure. You will notice that most of your systems are cryptic, hidden, or difficult to understand.

Technology cannot be this way if you are going to effectively implement real time interaction management as your new business capability. By tracking the source of decision-making behavior, changes can be noted, mapped, and implemented by your business in a fast and effective manner.

Your current capabilities will need to be explored at length by your IT team and the senior management in your company. Assess what your current systems can and cannot do, then see how you can go about changing them into interaction management systems that will contribute to your new customer-centric business culture.

Your Marketplace Comparison

It is no secret that businesses have been spending small fortunes on new technology that uses, processes, and manages data. Information management, data collection, quality integration, and reporting are all part of the business intelligence infrastructure they have been attempting to build.

Data that was once unused and hidden inside transactions can now be used to leverage sales and improve marketing effectiveness. Based on past interactions, these systems create a set of results that are then handed to analysts. These business analysts then study the data and make assessments based on the stored information.

So far, it is done a lot to help businesses get ahead. As you know, before any major system revamp, a market comparison must be looked at. Businesses that continue to only use past interactions to formulate future decisions will not be able to integrate sustainable decision management systems into their businesses.

When technology is making the decisions in decision management, no humans are present. Therefore no analysis can happen. Feeding historical data into a decision management system would be like trying to drive a motorcycle forward by gazing into the rear view mirror.

Product recommendation engines are powered by data, but data can be complex. There are two main categories that only e-commerce personalization programs know how to gather. If you only use one, you are only seeing half of your opportunity.

Your product recommendation engine needs to know how to listen. Pay attention to what your site visitors do. Think of it as a mystery that every customer click attempts to solve. These clues are called implicit data. The better your program, the clearer the mystery becomes, but you cannot only rely on implicit data to make recommendations. To make this data useful, it must be fed through analytic models that predict what the customer is going to do next.

As I do most of my shopping online, I have noticed many online retailers have adopted this capability very well and have begun to evolve it at an amazing rate. I think I first noticed it with Amazon.com as a new user about five years ago. In one of my initial interactions with the site, I noticed that as I clicked different items, the site began to make recommendations that were enticing to me. After I created an account and made a purchase, those recommendations became more and more precise. In fact, so much so that I now find myself shopping from the "recommended" products portion of the site just as much as I do from the direct searches I provide. It is no surprise that it is a highly profitable capability for Amazon, and other retailers have taken notice. In fact, it is difficult to find a major website that does not have this capability. From Homedepot.com to Walmart.com, your experience on their online assets is actively using RTIM in a way that is driving huge profitability in the form of incremental sales—a direct growth strategy.

The second kind of data is called explicit data, and it also powers your product recommendation engine. This is information that is gleaned directly from your site visitors—no guessing required. Connecting to a social profile, for example, gives your engine a better idea of who your client may be. With implicit and explicit data, your product recommendation engine is the best way to ensure increased sales conversions across the board.

Are you noticing how many new services online now allow you as a user to login with your Facebook.com account in lieu of registering manually? While it simplifies the registration process for you the user, the real benefit is for the company you are registering with. The data that flows from Facebook to that new website you are registering with is enough personal information to start presenting information that is specific enough to you that you will start to fulfill that new website's strategy. Most often it is trying to sell you something, but that is not always the case.

Backward looking data has its place, but it is not a primary focus in decision management systems. Systems cannot think for themselves; they can only act on the information that you give them. It makes sense, then, to provide your systems with analyzed data so that they can see a view of the future. That is why it is called predictive analytics, not past analytics!

Predicting likely future behavior is at the very heart of these progressive decision management systems in real time interaction management. You can imagine the immediate and long lasting "edge" that you will acquire from algorithms like these.

Positive and negative customer behavior predictions will give you the data you need to sell products to individuals based on past interactions and future potential interactions. These systems predict risk and fraud, opportunity, and the impact of decisions. When you combine this data, it makes for a powerful new way to sell more products to existing clients.

It is important to conduct a market comparison to see if your immediate competition has begun to leverage these decision management systems in their infrastructure. If they have, you should find it even more urgent to ready and prepare yourself for the design and implementation of your own real time interaction management systems.

If your immediate competition does not currently use decision management systems, then you have a unique opportunity to pull ahead—while they are still trying to make sense of the influx of past data. This is the competitive advantage that you can secure for your company during the implementation of this new system.

Data Quality and Complexity

The TIPP approach helps you approach the capability from a holistic view in an effort to uncover the potential of real time interaction management systems as you design, build, and integrate them into your business. TIPP addresses the multiple dimensions, or "lenses," in which to look at the interaction to ensure you are designing holistic interactions. As you know, the data quality and the simplification of business complexity will reach new heights with this system.

It is widely known in the business arena that poor quality data results in reduced business intelligence, or intelligence that is flawed and destined to fail. If your business does not prepare to deal with these existing issues, there will be unreliable strategies and tactics being proliferated throughout your company.

Data quality is a key risk that can jeopardize your business capability as all successful businesses must have quality data in order for these systems to work. Even if all other system capabilities are correct, if your data is unusable, you have a serious problem. Data holds to the "garbage in, garbage out" theory, which means that if your data is poor, you do not have to look closer at your technology interaction systems.

It is critical to first get your data architected and correct so that your real time interactions work. If you simply use garbage data, your interactions will also be garbage—and they can do more harm than good in almost every business case.

Business itself is becoming more complex with big data, multiple channels of engaging with your customer base, and products or offerings that are far from simple. Understanding the data that comes in from these foundation sources is critical. You design the intelligent interactions in your business, which is why it is important to get the data foundation evolution right—so that new capabilities can be accommodated.

Predictive analytics has been found to offer solutions to awkward customer behavior questions that have plagued sellers for years. Based on past and future behavior, your real time interaction management system will automatically offer products and services to individuals based on things they have bought and things they may want from your company.

As you can imagine, this is a revolutionary way to sell and operate a business. It is a progressive way to streamline your current systems so that they are able to adapt to customer behavior—guaranteeing more sales over time. Too many information systems have a single approach to decision making that is fixed and unmovable. This single approach is inflexible to someone looking at the data and physically making changes to the code of the system. These systems collect huge volumes of data, but they will not act on this data until a person comes in and makes these critical changes.

This is an outdated method of system development. If you are going to properly ready and prepare your business for interaction management systems, you cannot afford to focus on one analysis at a time, testing it, and then making a decision.

Good or bad decisions are effectively moving targets. There is constant change in customer decisions, which makes this field of study incredibly difficult to nail down. But as competitors, markets, and customer behavior shifts, the effectiveness of a decision is eroded.

That means that interaction management systems have to optimize their behavior over time, continuously refining and improving the way that they behave. You can say, then, that your interaction management system must continuously improve, test, and learn to be effective.

These systems have to know about decision making and collect data on it. They must, in essence, automatically improve their own view and skill when it comes to decision making and process execution. This is why we can say that when you implement or design your new real time interaction management system, you need a new approach to do it.

Interaction management is like building a brain that controls many different arms and hands that execute the vital functions in your business. Your human brain needs to learn how something is done first, and it is the same for interaction management systems. You will have to build this business capability one step at a time while optimizing each of the four pillars: technology, intelligence, people, and process. Your interaction management system will continue to learn and improve the actions and functions of the arms and hands it controls.

The TIPP approach will lead you through outdated interactions and show you a new way of creating and implementing your new intelligent interactions. While also setting the foundation for data quality and complexity available to you in this modern age, these new capabilities are possible.

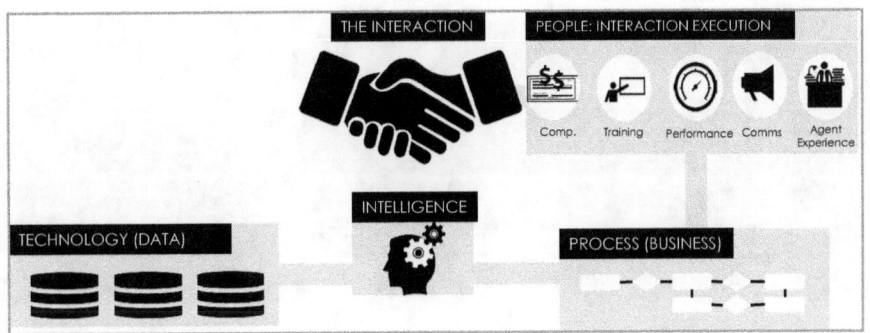

From a Technology "lens" we:

- Identified the business stakeholders that were current state "owners" for technology enablement for the specific contact channel(s) (desktops tools, online web presence and strategy, etc.) and partnered with them to educate them on the approach and to communicate the goals and objectives of the effort.
- Gathered a high level understanding of the data quality and structure that feeds current state "intelligence" to the current state processes.
- Identified the business stakeholders who were current state "owners" of the data assets that might be needed to be leveraged to create the new interaction.

- Partnered with them to educate them on the approach and to communicate the goals and objectives of the effort.

CHAPTER 4
Intelligence Readiness and Preparation

> *"BI [Business Intelligence] is about providing the right data at the right time to the right people so that they can take the right decisions."*
>
> NIC SMITH, MICROSOFT

At the heart of every modern, capable business is their ability to deal with data. The better your data sourcing, collection, and processing strategies, the stronger your business intelligence will become. In the future, it will be a race between the businesses that have learned to adequately read and use the information they have gathered.

Preparing for improved business intelligence means that you will have to determine where your current intelligence lies. You will also have to gain a more complex understanding of the new intelligence that you will be introducing into your business's daily processes.

How Data Quality and Complexity Result in Intelligence

Data quality and complexity are key to building reliable, dependable business intelligence systems. Your real time interaction management system is one such system that you need to ready your teams for.

Assessment is the real goal of any readiness and preparation exercise. In business intelligence, it serves to ground you in knowledge of the systems that you have, how your data works, and how it contributes to the higher functioning of your people and processes.

Simply having business intelligence systems is not good enough anymore, as I have been explaining to you throughout this book. Most intelligence is linked to sourcing and retaining new customers, which is not where your current focus should be directed.

Businesses with high volumes of data or extremely complex data need to be extra vigilant during this process as widespread errors can result in poor business intelligence and flawed goal setting. The good news, however, is that with real time interaction management—or intelligent interactions—the data is always top quality despite being complex.

Achieving data quality means that you will have to understand that quality is sourced by continuous processes and action. Practice, testing, and re-integration are at the very core of quality, complex data systems. This is what will result in business intelligence that exceeds your expectations. Correct the data, and your decisions can be made effectively.

Data quality programs will become a part of your new real time interaction management process once you have decided what you need, what to remove, and how to ensure your systems are continually improved.

Predictive Models and Advanced Analytics

It is no secret that the business market is experiencing a massive shift in business intelligence because of the rising need for information and progressive technology. The old model that once supplied businesses with data was called traditional analytics.

We can see that there is a large move from traditional to predictive analytics because the latter is based on the newer business intelligence that is aligned with customer-centric sales and experiences. For years analytics have given businesses the tools they need to analyze past and present sales trends. However, this outdated "past and present" data is no longer sufficient.

Now that businesses have changed from enterprise-centric interactions to customer-centric interactions, the future is more valuable than the past. Future data can help businesses profile individual customers and will see them predicting trends, behaviors, and patterns in an attempt to understand their key target markets better.

This is why advanced analytic systems will need to be developed and leveraged to remain competitive and earning income from existing clients. When you know who is entering and leaving the market and who is buying what, when, and how, it certainly gives you data to use to predict the future behavior of your buyers.

Traditional analytics tools have their place, but these do not provide your business with the FULL view that you need to make quality decisions. With only historical data on their side, what you are getting is a "rear" analysis of your customer base.

This is useful for tracking and monitoring past campaigns for improvement, but it does nothing to help you sell more products to that same customer in the future. This is the inherent problem with traditional analytics systems.

With predictive models and advanced analytics on your side, you will be able to determine the probable future outcome of an event. With the data mining techniques available today, predicting future trends and patterns is at your fingertips. With proper investment, these predictive models can be constructed to handle high volumes of data that are incredibly complex and varied.

If you can measure the trends, patterns, and behaviors of a statistically significant sample, theoretically, you have enough data to establish a foundation to start gleaning insights. Once you have a base of data to start with, you then begin to run structured experiments to refine and further test analytic accuracy. Using this approach will lay a decisioning dataset that will lend itself to operational decisions that will have a fairly reliable level of accuracy.

Imagine if your real time interaction management system could handle the data mining for millions of customers, providing your business with the predictive insight to upsell and cross sell more products and services to a wider global market.

With a combined microscopic and telescopic view of your data, you will be able to analyze and base decisions on minute details collected by your real time interaction management system. The right knowledge discovery will lead to the best decision making opportunities, which in turn will result in an overall increase of profit over time per customer.

The Power of Business Rules

In decision management right now, there is a growing trend towards business rules management systems. These support the practice of decision management and real time interaction management by automating and managing high volume transactional decisions. Business rules are very much like guard rails on a highway; they often represent the areas where you do not want your decision results to be made.

Keep in mind that decision management involves a focus on managing and automating select business decisions—like day-to-day operations—that do not require human input. Together with improved data quality, there is a need for new business rules to help manage the decisions that your team will make once the systems are implemented.

In an operational environment, your company will need a set of software components to create, test, manage, and maintain the new business rules that you implement. This is often called a "business rule engine."

This engine is one single part of a system that deals with the EXECUTION of a process; for example, an order process. Not all business rule systems have an engine; instead, they deal with development and testing of rules, linking rules to data, identifying conflicts and quality problems, and measuring how effective the new rules are for the business.

You will find that elements of decision logic management are supported by business rule systems. These systems support rules gained by optimization and analytics tools and rules created manually by the company.

Decision services are linked from the business rule management system to focus on managing decisions. A decision service is like an agent that you can call that has a view of all the data, actions, and conditions that have to be considered before an operational business decision can be finalized. In layman's terms, you will need a way to manage the architecture or blue print of each decision or rule, or series of rules, in an interaction. And you will need it for all interactions.

These decision services adopt behavior that is understandable to the business. They integrate historical data, have no side effects, explain decision execution, and support fast iteration without interruptions. On the whole, you should be using business rule management systems to help you build decision services.

If you do, this will translate to real power for your business. You will get design transparency, transparency when you are executing decisions, and collaboration. To get to the point where your business will be able to do this, you need to:

- Identify and model decisions that matter to your company by beginning with decision discovery.
- Create and build decision services by integrating business rule management into your systems so that you can get the decisions you need with one contact.
- Implement an analysis process for your decisions to guarantee that you are tracking and testing how your decisions are being made. The rules need to be kept up to date.

As you can see here, business rules are an essential part of decision making, and therein lies the real power. If you can make the right DECISION at the right TIME, you have the opportunity to rapidly affect business processes and greatly affect your bottom line.

The Types of Analytic Models Needed for Interactions

While there are different types of analytics that you may leverage as you build out your intelligent interaction system, the main focus when constructing the final output will be a predictive model. A predictive model is first and foremost a mathematical equation that collects data and produces information from it, like a number or score/odds ratio. Knowing this, there are several types of models used in business; namely descriptive models, decision models, and predictive models. When it comes to designing intelligent interactions, the predictive model is the type of model you will most likely leverage for your solution.

Predictive models are commonly designed to answer a particular business question. Typically, predictive models are built in a structured way. The process of constructing a predictive model usually starts with a hypothesis in mind. Building and testing the validity of a predictive model is very much like a designed experiment. In my experience, we would develop a predictive model very much in the same way we were taught in elementary school to design and develop a science project. You start with the "hypothesis" you are trying to prove, and as a result, you establish a null-hypothesis that is the opposite of your hypothesis. There is an "introduction" describing the overall intent of the experiment and what you are trying to prove. The next section in a model summary is the "methods" section that describes 1) the data techniques used to establish the data set and 2) the statistical procedures and tests that were executed throughout the model development process. The next section describes the "results" of the predictive model. "Results" speaks to the observations that were made throughout the model development. Finally there is a "conclusion" section that describes the final findings. The conclusion section describes the model's output in comparison to the initial hypothesis. It also describes how accurate the model is and any other significant observations throughout the process. At a very high level, predictive models can be constructed to answer just about any question you have data for with a varying level of quality depending on sample size. The questions a predictive model could answer may be things like, "Will this customer churn?" or "Will this customer be profitable?" or "What is this customer most likely to buy?"

One important thing to understand about predictive models is that they are not a one and done exercise. Over time, as more interactions occur and data changes, predictive models degrade in accuracy. To create a predictive business model that has a high degree of predictability, a continuous process of updating and recalibrating the model must always be in play to be effective. If you need to create a predictive model that will drive customer interactions, then you would begin by understanding the data, preparing it, modeling it, evaluating it, deploying it, and then monitoring and evaluating it. The cycle continues as this information is collected and decisions are made and implemented; then the process repeats.

A predictive business model is a statistical equation that analyzes data to predict how likely it is a particular customer will exhibit a particular behavior or action in the future. It encompasses a large variety of techniques, from machine learning, modeling, statistics, and data mining to the evaluation of past and present data. This information is used to "predict" unknown events.

Predictive models are used to greatly improve marketing practices but can effectively improve your business operations as a whole. In other words, they help sell your existing customer base more products and services and help the overall operations to run more efficiently, reaping more profit for the business in the end. These models are usually coupled with descriptive and decision models to make up what is called "Predictive Analytics."

The descriptive model, for example, quantifies relationship data to specifically classify customers into particular groups. While predictive models focus on the behavior of an individual, descriptive models bring to light the many different relationships between products and customers. These descriptive models are used to segment entities into different classifications. A good example of this would be how Delta Airlines is able to group their customers into different categories based on many different insights about a specific customer. Through this segmentation, they are able to classify customers based on Silver, Gold, Platinum, and Diamond statuses that all drive differentiated business processes depending on which segment or "type" of customer you are.

Decision models are used to define the relationship between all elements of your decision. This includes predictive model data, the core decision, and the predicted results of the decision. This is done to determine or "predict" the results of various decisions. They are used to optimize processes and reduce risk.

Collectively, these predictive, descriptive, and decision models make it possible to produce the information required in predictive analytics. You can then combine these analytics with decision management systems to create the desired outcome. When it comes to real time interaction management, the intelligence that comes from modeling and business rules is very much like the brain of the interaction, so the goal is to ensure that you have dedicated resources focused on constantly driving the intelligence of the interaction forward. Do not underestimate the complexity and resource investments you will need to make to get the intelligence dimension to a high degree of accuracy.

The application of predictive analytics is a very effective way to gain insights you otherwise would not have gotten. These powerful analytics have been used to improve customer relationship management, account collections, cross and upselling, decision support systems, fraud detection, risk reduction, underwriting, direct marketing, and product or market predictions. But understand that predictive models by themselves do nothing for the business; they must be acted upon, monitored, and refined to make lasting impact.

Your business needs to have these capabilities as you go about designing and building your real time interaction management systems. They are complex, but done correctly, they will usher in an unprecedented level of business intelligence that will transform the way you expand and earn income.

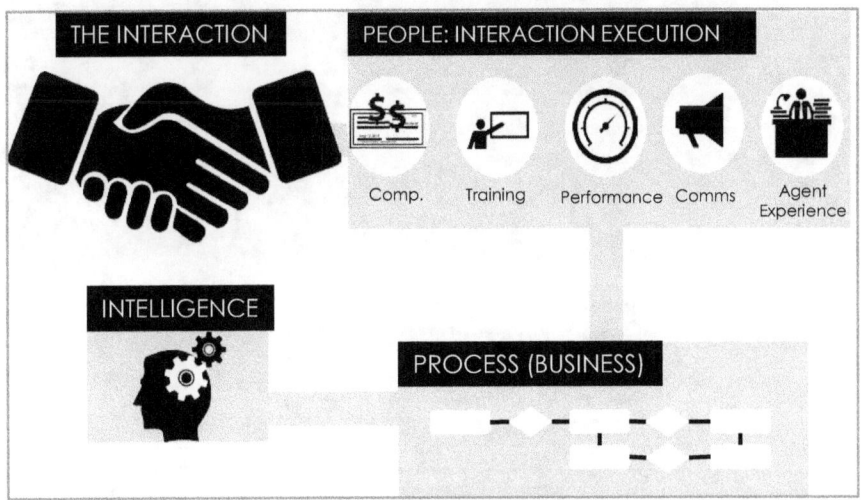

From an Intelligence "lens" we:

- Identified within the current-state business processes that we assessed where there were the largest opportunities for customer insights (segments to impact, customer value, risk to churn, etc.) that could map back to impact the strategic objective/ROI.
- Gathered an understanding of what current intelligence was being consumed by the current-state processes and got a basic understanding of the data and modeling sources of that intelligence.
- Gathered an understanding of which business stakeholder(s) "own" the current state intelligence modeling and analysis, and we partnered with them to educate them on the approach and to communicate the goals and objectives of the effort.

CHAPTER 5
Process Readiness and Preparation

> *"Measures that help decision makers define and measure progress toward business goals. KPI metrics translate complex measures into a simple indicator that allows decision makers to assess the current situation and act quickly."*
>
> **KAIZEN ANALYTICS**

The second last element in the TIPP approach to real time interaction management is the readiness and preparation of your business's processes. Everything in your business right now is governed by specific processes that have been developed over the years.

Sometimes these processes can exist for no reason. They simply exist because someone decades ago decided that their method was the right way to perform a certain task. These days we are able to measure process efficiency using specific key performance indicators (KPIs), which shed light on what needs to be done for improvements to occur.

The Current Process Measures and KPIs

- What is the level of transparency for key business processes?
- What are the key metrics that are derived that leadership and the business consider "important"?

There are thousands of metrics that are used in a business to measure certain parts of a business process but only a small handful that actually matter to your core business objectives. Those small handful of metrics are referred to as KPIs, or Key Performance Indicators.

When you design interactions, it is important to design and align interactions in a way that moves these KPIs (obviously in a positive way).

In your business right now, there are certain process measures and key performance indicators that you use to ensure that your organization operates smoothly.

- A KPI is a subset of metrics that your company will track and monitor in order to determine how well that process is doing.

In other words, these KPIs are used to measure business performance.

The current process measures in your company are most likely outdated. For example, your customer experience model may be virtually non-existent right now.

The reality is that your business must now deliver a branded, compelling, and profitable customer experience. There are different customer experiences for different customers based on their individual preferences. The value is not in cleverness but in execution—organizational engagement, IT changes, and process discipline.

How mature are your business processes? Do people follow a standard process or a specific business process across your organization? Is it measurable and enforceable? Is it non-standard and difficult to see the effectiveness of the business process? These are key questions that will help you understand your "current state" plan for the interaction process(es) that you will need to drive the targeted customer interactions.

- The process is the vehicle that will carry the interaction in a way that produces value, adding results in a consistent manner.
- Process maturity and execution will be a major factor in interaction consistency; if the process is "spotty," then you can assume the interaction will be equally as spotty.

When I talk about process, whether in the TIPP process or in another context, I am not only talking about the design and execution of a business process. I am touching on what I would call "business architecture." When I talk about process, I am not only talking about documenting processes but putting the organizational structure in place to execute, measure, and sustain the business process. This is sometimes called Business Architecture or Organizational Architecture/Design.

A basic process example would be the making of a sandwich. While there are millions of ways to make a sandwich, creating a standard process that leverages technology, people, and intelligence creates consistency, which in turn drives a customer experience.

- When you go to McDonald's, does the Big Mac ever look or taste like a Subway sandwich?
- Have you ever been to McDonald's and they have not been able to deliver a Big Mac?

The reason your sandwich is consistent is because there is a process they followed to make the sandwich. McDonald's has gotten so good at the processes surrounding their products that they can not only repeat the delivery of sandwiches in an extraordinarily efficient way but they can actually use intelligence to predict demand is such a way that ensures they will never run out of the pieces and parts that are required to make their products. Of course, there are anomalies, and they happen, but when I think about effective business process, McDonald's come to mind. McDonald's has become so good at its processes that they have KPIs across all parts of the overall process as well as sub processes that trigger different actions. Running low on cheese? The sub process triggers the order and delivery process for cheese. Summer time approaching? The intelligence behind the fulfillment process knows milkshake sales are about to increase, and all of the supporting processes execute.

But it was not always like this. McDonald's started with manual processes just like almost every business. Until you take a hard look at defining and implementing process in a standard way and then wrapping it with technology and fueling it with intelligence, you will always be executing manual processes that have the opportunity to be more efficient. Do you think McDonald's would be McDonald's without these consistent processes? Their processes are part of the secret that makes their customers' experience consistent around the globe.

Instead of one-sided conversation, your brand will proliferate contextual, dynamic, personalized, and intelligent conversations that support the concept of the "human metaphor." Your business is a virtualized human being, and customers expect conversations that are relevant, consistent, and controlled and those that contain choice and are dynamic.

When you implement real time interaction management systems, many of these process measures and KPIs will change for the better.

The TIPP approach accounts for all flavors of business processes. Whether customer facing processes or back office processes, understanding the linkage to the customer should be the focus as you begin to scope and prepare processes that will link to measurable interactions.

- Where do you currently stand within your organization?

Understand all processes within scope for the interaction you are looking to design that will be analyzed and potentially changed based on the strategy you are trying to implement and the customer experience you are trying to evoke, regardless of maturity.

This new capability will allow your business more transparency or visibility with business process than ever before. Today's technology not only shows you when a process fails but also shows you at what point in the process you are getting this "fall out."

What Gets Measured Gets Done

"What gets measured gets done. What gets measured and fed back gets done well. What gets rewarded gets repeated." – John E. Jones

The data age has arrived. Progress reports, evaluations, measures, data, and metrics are all part of growing a healthy business in this day and age. Business performance is what every company is after. It is accurate to say, then, that what gets measured gets done.

- What is getting done in your company?

People are told where to place their focus with incentives in the workplace. This directly correlates with these business processes that impact these key performance indicators and measurements. If you can understand the link between people and process, you can build interactions in that "sweet spot."

The challenge arrives when we are made to choose the metrics that really matter. If these can lead to sustainable gains, then that is a job well done. Performance has to be improved by effecting behavioral change in your workforce. Even though metrics almost always contain numbers, they often have very little to do with the way in which we measure certain KPIs.

Measurement is about understanding the cause and effect of a decision. It is about guiding and monitoring improvement towards a tangible goal. Using these metrics, you can reduce or eliminate problems and make way for improved human performance across the organization.

When your managers are consistently measuring the processes of your business and they are incentivized appropriately, they are almost guaranteed to improve over time. Measurement allows them to see the faults, risks, and opportunities that exist in the current process. Initially, these changes will be vast because you are transitioning to real time interaction management for the first time.

- Customer centric decisioning command and control will move from a non-existent or disjointed system of separate "control" centers to a single decisioning command and control center, which is far more effective.
- Customer relevance will move from product-push treatments to customer-relevant treatments. This will strike a balance between maximizing customer relevance vs. maximizing financial impact for your organization.
- Total customer intelligence will move from pockets of customer intelligence siloed by channel or process to one customer intelligence truth based on consistently updated systems.
- Empowered customer facing front lines will move from strictly scripted monologues to intelligence supported dialogues.
- Centralized customer facing decisions will move from fragmented decision engines to a single decisioning engine.
- Customer centric management will move from siloed optimization across channels and processes to centralized optimization across channels and processes.

These moves that are made are purely due to the new process

KPIs that are measured consistently over time. As information comes to light, the processes are adapted, changed, reviewed, and improved. The result is a far more reliable system of process measurement.

What Is the State of Business Process?

New processes may need to be developed to support the implementation of interaction management systems. Two important processes that you will need to evaluate are how you maintain your decision inventory and how you manage your software development lifecycle.

- Do you know if your business processes are consistent, transparent, measurable, immeasurable, or inconsistent?

They need to be aligned to performance metrics. That is why you have to know whether they are cross functional or functionally siloed. Which people in your organization manage and enhance these processes? These are all vital questions to ask at this point.

A capability maturity model like BPMM[10] (or business process maturity model) allows managers to describe the current state of an enterprise from the process management maturity perspective. Using this model, you should be able to describe the current state or current strengths and weaknesses in your business, determine the desirable maturity level depending on key factors of business process management, and make BPM easier to improve with maps that show how to reach this desired state.

Currently, many organizations have not adopted the use of multiple data-model views. They still use the same model for service design, process variables, and business rules. But decision management systems have more data elements than almost any

---

10 Marija Andjelkovic Pesic, Business Process Management Maturity Model and Six Sigma: An Integrated Approach for Easier Networking, http://emnet.univie.ac.at/uploads/media/Andjelkovic-Pesic_01.pdf

single business process can manage.

Different or multiple business processes need to be implemented in order to effectively manage a decision management system. There are many businesses that prefer to create "across-the-board" processes to standardize good ideas. Single enterprise information models are easier to set up, although there is nothing wrong with this system—except that it becomes nearly impossible to measure.

How do you go about measuring or determining the business value of an enterprise-wide effort? It is no wonder so many of these initiatives fail! It is great to have an enterprise-wide decision inventory, but to try and create it all in one project is not a best practice.

The state of your current business processes will likely not be adequate when you implement real time interaction management systems. As I explained before, when you standardize a process and introduce it on an enterprise-wide scale, measuring it is often very difficult, but it does not have to be.

These are some of the potential process challenges that you will face, so it is great that you are familiarizing yourself with them now. Collaboration, as always, is also important to interaction and decision discovery as it takes shared responsibility between IT, business stakeholders, and analytics teams to keep it aligned and updated.

Creating Cross-Functional Leadership Buy-in

Your management teams will need to be the dominant force behind this new process implementation. In addition, there is only one way you can effectively get these three very different teams to work together. It is called cross-functional communication, and it involves gathering key leaders from various departments together so that they can work together to create "whole" solutions for the organization.

Instead of the old model that used an entire IT team to create a process, you will be using this cross-functional leadership structure to approach your decision management processes from the top down. It is focused on the whole solution, which includes technology, analytics, and the business operations of the company.

Most commonly these cross functional "teams" or stakeholders collectively represent the entire organization's interests within the defined project; in this case, for real time interaction management. The real question is—How do you get these opposing teams working together? How do you get them to buy into the concept of cross-functional leadership?

- Establish an owner that is committed across functional boundaries to care and feed the natural business processes (garden keeper).
- The process owner needs to manage some, or all, of the resources engaged in the process.
- They need to act as a process decision maker and ensure the efficiency, consistency, and sustainability of the process.
- They should review reports on performance metrics and ensure the progress toward standardization and improvement.
- The process owner needs to jointly manage the process team and the ongoing quality assurance and change management associated with the process.
- They need to communicate progress and results to stakeholders.

Constant collaboration: Ensuring that all the various leadership groups involved are engaged in the creation of the decision inventory will improve its quality and keep them all working together for the greater good of the overall system.

Reworking new projects: Every new project should reuse existing decision inventory content and add new content to it effortlessly. When the time comes to reuse existing content, or create new content, it is important that all of the stakeholder's leadership teams participate.

Interaction Ownership – Targeting Accountable Candidates

As a business owner or senior level executive, it is your responsibility to be directly involved in the interactions of your organization. It is only when senior management is intimately involved that you can capitalize on your human and capital assets.

Targeting accountable candidates to help you lead your business into the 21st century by implementing real time interaction management is essential to its success.

Someone needs to own EACH interaction. Since TIPP is about creating a specific interaction, someone will need to own the specific components around the interaction. It could be the same person that owns the process—or it may not be—but someone will need to own the interaction (all pieces), or the interaction will become stale and will eventually fail.

A person within the organization who knows that the object is to define and apply accountability in a way that ensures the interactions you create will get leadership support and resources in the future.

ROI: What Is the Business Case for Interaction Management?

The final priority for your business has to be your business ROI strategies. Results should be where this entire system focuses and ultimately excels. I like to call it "the performance frontier" because it is where most businesses focus their energy these days.

Your organization's business ROI strategies need to come first—no matter what new system you are creating or new method you are implementing. A good ROI is the glue that binds project investments to organizational results. You have to systematically predict, measure, and manage your interactions to gain that competitive advantage.

You are not in business to make customers like you; you are in business to make money. Every investment that is made in business should have some kind of "return" of benefit to the business. RTIM systems are a big investment, and there needs to be a significant return. Because you are investing heavily in people, process, intelligence, and technology, it is critical to directly link these designed interactions to areas where your business will get the most return.

If you examine the interaction opportunities, it will be important to identify the largest opportunity and attempt to apply an interaction to that opportunity in a way that gives your business a return. Return can equate to increased revenue, better net promoter scores, longer customer retention, or lowering the cost to serve a specific segment of customers.

The point is that you should never take your eye off the "return." It is critical that you focus on ROI from the beginning as this will be the proof that you need to justify your investment, and it will become the leverage you need to continue getting your company to invest in the capability.

The business case for interaction management is really that it consistently improves return on investment for a number of your evolving business processes. When your business processes are able to improve so can your decision management systems. At the end of the day, your real time interaction management system will be on target if you take a deliberate focus on the TIPP approach. Overlooking any one area, especially business process, will greatly increase the chances of failure.

Be upfront about what you intend to accomplish with RTIM, and communicate it across the organization. Even if you do not hit your target, that does not equal fail unless you let it. Again, the TIPP framework is a test and learn methodology that will sometimes not be exactly what you target. The idea is to learn from your efforts and evolve them until you do hit the right mix of TIPP in the interactions you want to design.

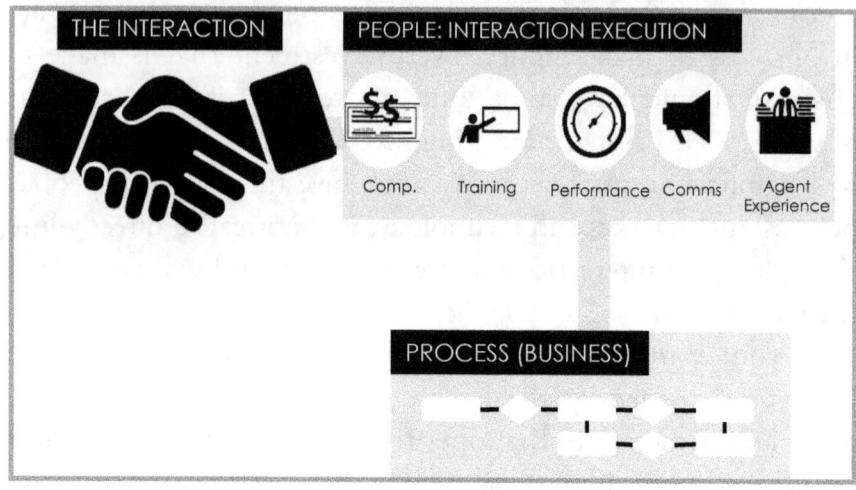

For the Process "lens" we:

- Gathered an understanding of what current customer facing and back office processes are most likely contributing to the challenges that are impacting the targeted business objective.
- Identified the business "owner" of the current state business process and partnered with them to educate them on the approach and to communicate the goals and objectives of the effort.
- Established clear linkage from processes in scope to the "interaction owners" goals and objectives.
- Gathered and analyzed current KPIs and metrics that provide visibility into the current state process and gathered an understanding of how "effective" current state is and where opportunities might be.

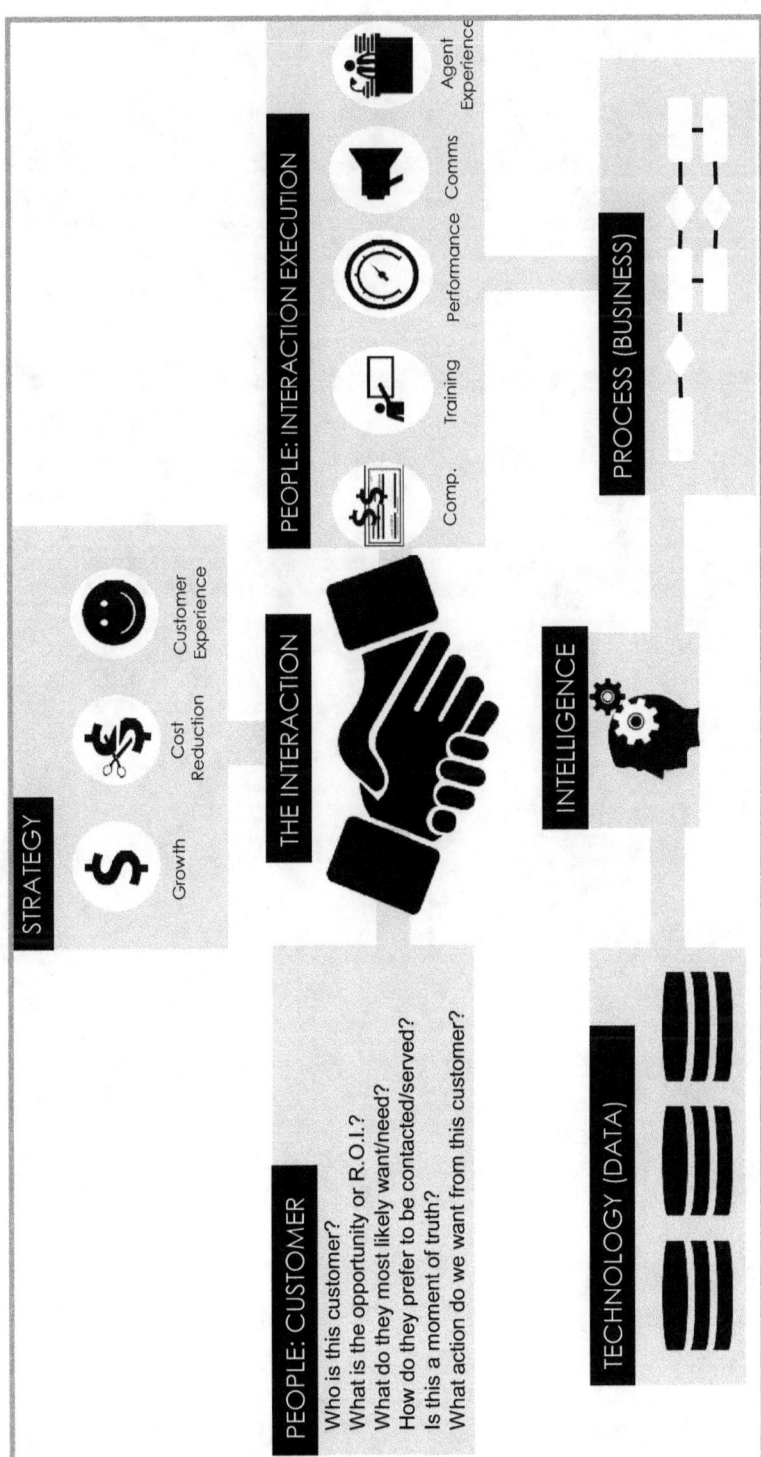

CHAPTER 6
People Readiness and Preparation

"To be a leader, you have to make people want to follow you, and nobody wants to follow someone who doesn't know where he is going."

JOE NAMATH

Technology is often thought of as the vessel for change, but the truth is that technology still needs people to make it work, and these systems are no different. This is why preparing all the levels of people in your organization for the creation and implementation of real time interaction management systems is fundamental to the success of the project as well as long-term sustainment. Success of RTIM starts at the highest levels of the organization. If your journey into RTIM starts anywhere less than a C-Level executive driving the effort, STOP! You will need buy-in at the highest levels of your organization to drive the type of transformation that will be needed in this journey. Ideally, you will have multiple C-Level executives supporting the effort.

Business people, IT people, and people that focus on data analysis are all key players in this transition. These are the leaders that will help your company correctly implement these new systems so that they are able to adequately optimize your business processes. You must have all three sets of people aligned with the C-Level support, or your chances of failure will increase exponentially.

As you begin to design the interaction(s) that will drive profitability to your business, I want to make one distinction in the "people" portion for the rest of this book. While there are two very distinct types of contact channels—human vs. non-human—in my experience, the more challenging contact channels have been human-based channels. Most likely because of exactly that, you are dealing with change and humans. In non-human channels, the website, mobile app and/or IVR system is not resistant to change, they are not upset when you negatively impact their compensation, and further, they do not complain when they get fired because you negatively impacted their performance metrics by designing your interaction in a way that did not contemplate them. For that reason, as we talk about "people" as it relates to TIPP going forward, I will more often be referring to the human contact channels as those are often the most delicate and hardest to do. Online experience interactions are also hard, but in my experience, you can get a direct customer interaction correct, and you can package those learnings and accelerate development into non-human contact channels.

RTIM Effectiveness Begins With Leadership Education and Commitment to Funding

Chances are most if not all of the leaders in your business do not have a clear understanding of what RTIM is. Having seen this leadership knowledge gap wipe out significant investments of time and money, I stress that leadership alignment and buy-in is just as important to your success as data quality is to effective decisions. In order to effectively build and sustain this capability within your business, leadership must understand what it is and, more importantly, how to use it to accomplish their strategic goals. Real time interaction management begins with training and educating your leaders on how to get out on the court and, more importantly, how to drive the right actions for the business. Training the business operations leadership should be an ongoing activity. Leaders will change over time, and nothing can stifle the progress made around implementing this business capability like a new leader that does not understand or see the value.

Leadership will need to be aligned and committed to funding this new business capability. One way you can set the effort up for success and long-term sustainment comes down to "Who is adjusting the interactions controls?" When it comes to building the interaction controls that will need periodic adjustments, it is better for long-term sustainment to build the management of interaction controls on the business operations side of the company. Build the resources and organization needed to adjust decisions and processes in the company on the business operations side of the house, and do not rely on technology to do the daily work. Technology will still have a role, but the day-to-day activity should be managed by the business. Why is that you may ask? Well, in my experience, it really comes down to funding. Technology needs capital function, or CAPEX, which is in opposition to business resources that are an operational expense, or OPEX. Ongoing support and funding will result in adjustments that need to be made in an OPEX world vs. CAPEX funding. CAPEX funding falls away when the project ends, which is usually when the "slow, painful death" process begins for these initiatives. That is why funding and day-to-day management matters way in advance. Get this wrong and it could result in a significant amount of rework as you try to course correct.

Business Transformation and Education

When building RTIM as a business capability, it is critical to understand that this is not just another business and/or technology project; this is business transformation at its core! Just like leaders need to be educated and understand the benefits and the driving force behind why the business has chosen to commit to RTIM, all levels in the organization must also understand. When you leave pockets of people throughout the organization that are not informed or educated, you run the risk of forming pockets of resistance. Chances are you will already have a few pockets of resistance to diffuse anyway, so there is no need to set yourself up for failure by overlooking the people you will need to support you just by forgetting to educate them.

Ongoing education is key. As resources change and as projects evolve, there will always be an ongoing need to educate your business on the capabilities of RTIM and how it is improving the business as well as future opportunities and capabilities that are coming down the road. Not only do I recommend having a resource accountable for training and education within your project team, but for the ongoing operations, it will be critical for the business to provide this education. Let's face it; businesses change, leaders change, resources change. The knowledge gaps around this capability will cause unnecessary pain and frustration.

In the near future, every business will need to focus on the core principles of transformation and education if they want to prepare for the integration of new technologies into their company. Real time interaction management is simple enough to maintain, but to integrate something this new and complex into an older system is going to take time and patience.

The people-centric part of your organization will need to step up at this point. All information systems need efficient collaboration between business people and their technology departments to function well.

You could say, then, that in order for transformation to take place, the correct level of education must be implemented in your workplace. You will need this kind of close collaboration to keep your systems working, for these reasons:

- All decision management systems make business-based decisions. Even the small decisions can result in a greater impact on the business as a whole. The business drives what constitutes a good or bad decision. In other words, your business leaders need to understand what actions, logic, policies, and regulations must be adhered to on a daily basis.
- Interaction management systems can also require systems that have been based on the business's strict policies and regulations. This involves the use of analytics to predict things like opportunity, fraud, or risk. All decisions need to be analyzed, even when predictive models are not required.
- Decision management systems mainly focus on low-latency, high-volume decisions. These are the decisions that must be made quickly and often on a day-to-day basis. Automation is key to this happening. That means IT needs to be a part of the system to supply additional data and foundational support as decisions are integrated into your transactional environment.

The real transformation will happen when these three teams begin to work together for your common business goals. Traditionally, in my experience, they are awful at working together in a business context—with many issues that have separated them over the years. They all have different focuses that they have been adhering to for decades.

Now, of course, both transformation and education depend on their ability to put this aside and collaborate for the greater good of their organization.

RTIM Capability Ownership Explained

Who owns the interaction platform as a business capability? The owner of the business needs to be cross functional by nature. If they reside in a single function, the capabilities will be used to support that function's goals and not the customer experience or other functional goals. For example, if you allow the interaction platform to be owned by marketing, you run the risk of the interactions being heavily skewed toward making an advantage for marketing. If you give the ownership of the platform to say a group that spans functions like, say, Business Operations or a Customer Experience organization, then they will partner across organizations more effectively as they do not have as much motive to use the platform to serve a single functions bidding. As a platform owner is identified, understand that they need to be committed to extending capabilities across customer touch points and should supply the resources needed to perform most (or all) of the following on the business side of things:

- Business rule management across the platform
- Create reusable decisions and interactions across touch points
- Ongoing education, leadership, and business execution, along with education technology on the benefits they experience
- Fight for funding when a new major development is needed like a new customer facing exposed channels, new upgrades for the platform, or new modeling capabilities

The idea is to have one group in your organization that handles the issues mentioned above, though any function can leverage the platform. RTIM is like a garden. The RTIM owner cares for the platform and supplies resources (common plants, fertilizer, extending the garden to new areas based on where opportunities lie—more sun, water, nutrients, etc.). The business functions come to the garden and plant their plants (objectives and goals) anywhere in the garden as long as they care for and feed their portion of the garden. It should look something like this:

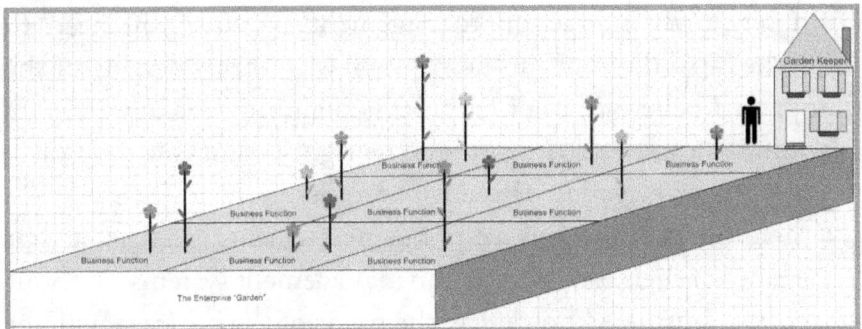

In business, there are both horizontal and vertical functions. Vertical organizations include each of your functional silos: sales, marketing, product development, customer care, training, and technology. These groups should have access to an enterprise garden but should not have their own function-specific garden. They need to be represented—by a cross functional team—but they are not good candidates to own the overall capability. They will build the capability to a very narrow focus that serves their needs and leaves out the other functional groups and customer needs.

Examples of horizontal organizations include customer experience organizations, business operations, and enterprise-wide business process organizations. Once you have identified the organization that owns the capability, you will need to identify a single owner who is as high up in the organization as possible. Identifying this person as early as possible is a huge accelerator in the long term.

Overlooking this step may result in some frustrated discussions when you try and find a "garden keeper" that is not really interested in gardens. I have seen this capability thrive when functions have the ability to use this capability but do not have to do the entire job of keeping it sustained. When you select a cross functional owner, it fosters team work across functions for goal achievement, and when it comes down to it, everyone wins—especially the customer.

A business capability is what an organization needs to be able to DO to execute a successful business strategy. They combine people, process, and technology in order to reach a strategic goal.

In real time interaction management systems, you need to align the capabilities of this new system with the ownership of the company. I believe that all IT process planning or analytics data planning is a waste of time unless the right business leaders own, and are fully engaged in, this entire process.

There are reasons why your business leaders need to accept ownership of these new interaction management systems. Without the correct business knowledge, the needs of the business will not be integrated into the system. This knowledge is critical to having aligned technology and analytics solutions that map to business process.

All technology capability objectives and analytics capability objectives need to be overseen by an interested leader. Otherwise, there will always be faults in the system that could have been avoided as the different teams work towards different, and separate, organizational goals. The business needs to benefit after all, not the departments in the business.

The leadership always needs to be engaged so that business capabilities align with the focus of both the IT and analytics departments. Planning takes time. It is another reason to keep the leadership of the business involved in the process. Technology, analytics, and even business processes are changing at an alarming rate, and leaders need to understand and support these changes. But the IT staff will only be aware of the changes in the IT field. They will know nothing of the changes in the analytics department or in your overall business processes and business operations. Working together and collaborating in the field of real time interaction management then becomes an essential—and a constant.

Planning and preparation should not be seen as a static, time-limited process. Even though plans are discussed and developed between the multiple teams, this is an on-going process due to the rapid changes that are always happening in each department of the business.

To properly build and implement decision management systems that work, the leadership of your business needs to be intimately involved. If you focus on decision discovery, your business results will improve alignment. Moreover, all organizational issues will be recognized and dealt with as they arise. The result is a constantly updated system that works.

What Drives Your Business Today?

There has been a fair amount of discussion around enterprise-centric businesses and where their core focus lies. If you pick up any business book these days, it will tell you that business is not about the product or service; it is about the customer, and then it is about what the people in your company are driving toward as it relates to the customer.

When they understand their roles in your business, you are able to create talent and process maps that will influence the entire future of the leadership in your company. Investing in people, along with a calculable change strategy, is the way of the future.

It becomes very important when you broach the topic of decision management systems, where close collaboration is key for overall success. Imagine spending a lot of time and money on your real time interaction management systems without readying and preparing your staff or department leadership for it—it just will not work.

Understanding what drives your company is key to aligning interactions to those specific drivers. Knowing how people are compensated or rewarded based on company performance will help. The factors that drive your business are typically aligned with the incentives that people work toward.

That means if your company if focused on growth, regardless of the business cost—and people's incentives are aligned to that strategy—your efforts will die a slow and painful death if you attempt to drive interactions to the contrary. If you are not directly supported by main incentives that people receive, you will confuse your employees—especially if the interaction you design actually takes money out of their pockets.

Conflicting with incentives is the fastest way to stifle end user adoption. These are not "build and they will come" systems; they require people alignment to make them work. To do that, you need to understand what the people in your organization are working towards.

While sales was once the only thing that mattered to enterprise-centric companies, clearly this is no longer the case. People have become the fundamental element that drives success. The right IT manager will guarantee that your technology capabilities are always updated and top notch.

They will take care of problems as they arise with your automated systems and will keep your IT staff working towards a unified goal. Your analytics manager will do the same on their end. Then, at the core of it all, are your business managers. These people will ensure that the IT manager and the analytics manager are working towards the needs of your business.

After all, operational efficiency is at the heart of any complex data system. Now that you have decided to plan, create, and maintain decision management systems in your company, it is the people that will determine whether or not your move will be successful.

Even though direct sales and sourcing new customers used to be your business's primary driving force, it is ignorant to believe that it will stay like this forever. We have completely moved over to a people-centric view of business that works even better—thanks to developing technology, process, and analytics solutions.

Your company leadership, staff, and customers are what matter now. It is the reason you are even learning about real time interaction management. Keep this in mind when you transition, and you will be all right. Do not underfund the compensation/incentive alignment analysis as well as the change management and education of the people in your business, or your system will suffer.

What Are the Biggest Challenges Your Business Is Facing?

There are dozens of challenges that your business will face during this transition period, and many of them will be people-centric. It is important that you get an idea of what you will be dealing with so that you can make provision to reduce or eliminate most of the core challenges before they arise.

- *Lack of communication between your stakeholder departments.* You need to get a dialogue going between your IT team, analytics team, and business stakeholder teams. They need to work together to identify decisions—both good and bad—so that accurate choices can be made based on all the facts.
- *Focusing on decision discovery.* Many believe that you can simply move directly into designing and building decision services, but there are many benefits to focusing on decision discovery first. First and most important it requires the business to think through and identify the strategy it is trying to accomplish and what strategic business objectives it is trying to accomplish as well as promote collaboration and get alignment from the cross-functional stakeholder and support teams to ensure feasibility.
- *Lack of collaboration skills.* It is essential that stakeholder groups work on their collaboration skills. They will each have conflicting points of view due to their past experience of what matters in their department. Cross training is important so that they can realign their goals and work together to achieve them.

- *Lack of focus on business results.* Each department will need to collaborate to realign their personal and organizational objectives. Everyone should be measured based on the impact that the decision management system has on the overall business results during production. They will not be measured on an individual system functioning or department efficiency.

One of the largest challenges that you will face are the individual issues that arise in each department on a day-to-day basis. You will have to implement a reporting system that each department can use, which will resolve organizational dysfunction and prevent them from drifting apart. These reports need to be read and acted upon by the department leadership.

Identify the reporting structure that each person in the project will use. Then make sure that the leadership understands the purpose and benefit of creating and working through these reports. This is how you maintain an excellent decision management system with cross functional teams that struggle to work together.

Location is another problem that large companies have as sometimes the IT department can be housed in another building or geographic area. Most of the time, these stakeholder departments are not logistically close to each other. It makes setting meetings and getting a hold of the right reports a hassle. You must designate a meeting cadence and drive toward cross functional alignment at least once or twice a week. Constant contact goes a long way when teams are collaborating.

Understanding Current Organizational Strategy and Objectives

Do you know what your company's current "hot button" may be? What C-Level executive is accountable for those challenges? Are they currently supporting you? If you can focus the first set of interactions around these questions, it can result in a very successful outcome. Perhaps there is a new competitor taking your market share, or you are experiencing loyalty problems, or the cost to serve in your service center is blowing apart your operational expense budget—RTIM can do all these things and more if you can get support from the organization. Rally to tackle the hottest, most pressing issues in your business that everyone is facing. This is key to generating RTIM momentum.

Current organizational strategy and objectives in your business are probably completely different to the ones outlined in this book. As previously mentioned, momentum needs to be created around hot topic capabilities if true alignment is to take place. This will be a considerable shift for your staff as they rally to implement these new crucial capabilities in your company.

With real time interaction management, you will have a new capability to achieve organizational strategies and objectives at the transaction level. Most likely your leadership will not completely understand the significance of this capability or will not have trust in it. This means, in preparation, you should strongly consider developing an educational overview for your stakeholder department teams to clearly understand "what RTIM is'" and, more importantly, what it is "not." As you target the stakeholders to educate, never forget that the managers in each department as well as the front-line staff will play a direct role in the future adoption of this capability. It will also impact your potential to leverage it to accomplish one to many operational strategies.

Organizational change needs to occur before new strategies and objectives can be met. It is usually a mistake to treat decision management systems as "just another project." If it is implemented or designed incorrectly, organizational dislocation can result.

- Managers could end up feeling less important as they no longer have to offer their approval for certain processes. The system will manage these approvals instead. Or inversely, they may now have new responsibilities that seem like more work to them, and they need to understand why these new responsibilities are important to them and the business.

- Staff on the frontline feel more responsible for the success of the system but feel their "chain of command" may not be effective if problems arise.
- Your call center and branch staff will have their customer options limited by the system to the point where they feel like they have no control.
- Customers will notice changes as features like personalized pricing come into effect—one of the benefits of decision management systems. However, the front line reps may not be able to effectively explain the logic in detail.
- The IT department will constantly worry that the decision management system will not remain stable because of the involvement of business managers that may have alternative agendas or lack what IT considers acceptable skills to manage the system.
- In the beginning, customers and staff may not trust the systems decisions even though they will have to accept it.

Current organizational strategy and objectives are based on separate departments performing their set functions in order to achieve a desired result. This needs to shift to a unified collaboration between the most important parts of your company: IT, analytics, and cross-functional business stakeholders. This is the tripod that will keep your business standing in the coming years.

Nearly all of your business strategies and objectives will change because of decision management and real time interaction management systems. It is a big shift but one that cannot wait any longer. It is going to place a significant amount of pressure on your people—as they are the driving force behind the success of this system.

This is why readiness and preparation is a key part of the pre-planning phase. When you educate your people, they are better equipped to pass on this education to the other staff members. As a whole, each department becomes more suited to making decisions based on your new organizational strategies and objectives. They will begin to focus and operate on a level that is broader than their own departmental and functional objectives.

Continuous Business Education – A New Way Forward

RTIM is evolving at an alarming rate, which is why you need to align people to monitor the changes that occur across the globe as well as within your marketplace.

With the ever changing markets that your business has to adapt to (new technologies) and the individual changes that occur on a micro-basis every day in IT (test and learn systems), analytics, and business, it is no wonder that the only way forward is through continuous education for your leadership and business.

In the past, it was acceptable to study and then learn all you needed to "on the job." Now, with the growth rate of new information and technology rising every minute, there is no way your business can remain current and optimized if you do not utilize the new concept of *"continued business education."*

- Continued business education for the senior leadership of your company must be integrated into your new systems as soon as possible.

Companies use technology, data mining, and predictive analytics to do it, but essentially, it is still a very human concern. At the very top level, education needs to be proliferated on a grand scale. You may encounter resistance to change and a reluctance to move over to this new system, but this is the system that will save your company in the coming years.

- Continuous business education means that everyone needs to be properly trained to work with, understand, use, and fix the system if need be. Real time interaction management systems are only as good as the people in charge of them.

Systems may know to update themselves in general, but people have to add in the complex bits.

This is why if your staff are prepared, your new system will run smoothly. Business is changing—from the grass roots level all the way up to the CEO and Board of Directors. I say that continuous education is the new way forward, but really it is *the only way forward* if you are going to be successful.

Just a few months can pass by, and without constant vigilance, your systems could become outdated and less effective. This means that without even realizing it, many of your customers could drift over to another brand, losing you sales and revenue. This reality will only multiply as time wears on.

- Customer loyalty is fragile and needs to be nurtured all of the time.

Invest in continuous education programs, conferences, workshops, webinars, course materials, meetings, and company-wide improvements in technology and business process that can help you easily disseminate new, applicable information at the click of a button. With the right systems in place, continuous education does not have to be costly.

Understand that this capability is evolving faster than anything we have seen in the competitive arena; if you and your business do not stay in touch and leverage the wisdom of others (even your competition), you will blink, and the hopes of staying in the race may soon be over for you.

For the People "lens" we:

- Identified the appropriate stakeholders and partnered with them to educate them on the approach and to communicate the goals and objectives of the effort.
- Focused and assessed the contact channel(s) where the interaction might be executed (this can and often does change)
- For human channels (call center / brick and mortar environment), began to understand the environment of the customer facing representatives that would potentially execute the interaction you wish to design. We gathered the current state of incentives, performance measures, most receptive method of communication (how they like to be contacted and most likely respond), how they are communicated to today (newsletters, team emails), current training levels, and current environment (desktop tools, knowledge systems)

PART III
Creating TIPP Designed Real-Time Interactions for Your Business

CHAPTER 7
Prioritizing Customer, Agent, and Business

"One customer well taken care of could be more valuable than $10,000 worth of advertising."

JIM ROHN

As you begin to design TIPP-enabled real time interactions for your business, you will need to address various experiences as they relate to your customers, agents, and business employees. Experience is really the true test of success in any interaction.

At this stage, you will need to prioritize which parts of your real time interaction management systems will make the most impact on your business. All experience is an investment on the part of your business, and it is your responsibility to ensure that each interaction produces the right experience that drives the most ROI-impacting result.

Customer Interaction Lifecycle

There has been a lot of research into the real impact of prioritizing customer interaction experiences recently with Forrester[11] stating that improved experiences can push a paltry $46 million to $1.7 billion in revenue—depending on the industry.

Clearly, it is important that you make customer interaction experiences a priority in your business as you start to design your real time interaction systems. If you focus on driving the right customer interaction with the right customers, you will be able to align your customer experiences with your brand promises by implementing the correct business processes.

Your goal is to develop a lifecycle or framework of the customer's relationship that results in repeat business, referrals, and profitable connections over an individual's lifetime that drive the ROI impacts you prepared for. As we know, all customers are different and are driven by different factors. However, that does not mean you cannot look at the "typical" past and present customer and begin to break their relationship with you into phases. This framework will prove to be invaluable as you will use it very much like a farmer uses lifecycle to take crops from seed to harvest. For a customer lifecycle, it might look something like this:

1. *Acquisition:* During the acquisition phase, efforts are really geared toward getting as many prospective customers as possible to look at your business's products and/or services. This is typically a marketing centric phase, where specific customers are messaged and promoted to. In this phase, the prospect becomes a new customer.

2. *Onboarding:* In this phase, there is some sort of activity around welcoming your new customer to doing business with your company. In this phase, there will be some sort of

---

[11] Megan Burns. The Business Impact of Customer Experience, 2010. http://www.forrester.com/rb/Research/business_impact_of_customer_experience,_2010/q/id/57617/t/2

education concerning your products and services. Just like farming, this is the most volatile time of the relationship. This phase includes the way that you manage the welcoming of a new customer and how you begin your relationship with them. Identifying risks that may drive them to churn and mitigating those activities is paramount during this phase.

3. ***Developing:*** As time goes on, the customer has purchased from you once, maybe multiple times. In a service organization, the customer may be an existing subscriber. During this phase, analysis and evaluation of the customer occurs to understand what, if anything, out of your catalog of product or services would benefit you as well as the customer based on the relationship so far. This is usually a good place to introduce other offerings for the customer via cross-sell / upsell opportunities.

4. ***Collections:*** At some point, the customer may fall into a collections phase, meaning they may have run into timeliness of payment issues. In this phase, selling the customer more product of service is probably not a good idea since they are not able to pay the current bill. This phase is usually a good place to understand the customer's value to the organization to see how much credit or investment the business is willing to make to save the specific customer.

5. ***Retention:*** In this phase, the customer is potentially leaving you. Perhaps they are not happy with your products or services, or in some cases, you might not be happy with their contribution to your bottom line. In either case, in this phase, it is very important to understand the specific customer's value and profitability and really understand just how much or little they play into your future.

6. ***Winback:*** In this phase, the customer churned, but you realize they were a good customer that got away. In this phase, you usually drop your guard and try to "woo" the customer

back, usually at a deeper discounted rate. In this phase, understanding how likely the customer is to come back and the likelihood they will stay is important to understand.

While this is just an example of a customer lifecycle framework and may be nothing like the one your business leverages, let us take a moment to see this complexity. Just looking at this lifecycle framework, can you picture all of your existing customers and where they are at any given point? Can you currently leverage that information at the point of contact to make the best interaction possible? If not, you are not alone. Guess what? This is how your business will be able to "cultivate" the existing customer base for maximum yields. Customers today expect that you know more about them; in fact, in today's marketplace, they demand it. As you can imagine, for each customer, there is a strong possibility that they are all in different phases in their lifecycle. Compound that with the fact that each customer has different needs and is contributing different things to your bottom line, and how will you ever figure out how to interact with them to drive the best customer experience? That is what the TIPP approach is all about. By designing one interaction at a time and not just taking broad strokes like "selling" or "servicing" interactions, you can contemplate the interaction from multiple angles to increase your likelihood of driving the right end result. This approach requires precision in design and execution as well as ongoing refinement

Knowing which customers you are looking to target and, more importantly, what phase they are in in their lifecycle will help you build the right interaction for the right person at the right time. Without this understanding of lifecycle, once again using the farmer analogy, you run the risk of trying to harvest customers well before their time and missing the harvest, or you wait too long and again you miss the opportunities to harvest, and you lose the crop.

Agent Interaction Experience

For human channels, again, call centers, brick and mortar stores, etc.: In many companies today, the frontline agent or end user is already living in a chaotic world. They have been thrown less than effective tools, broken processes, and meaningless metrics and literally live in a world of frustration with everything being a top priority. If you hand them this capability with contemplating the environment that they already live in, this will become just another "flavor of the day."

In the planning phase, you assessed how the frontline agent's environment (desktop experience, knowledge base, business processes, and measurements) is currently impacting the area where you wish to implement RTIM. When you deliver this to the front line, if it is perceived and designed as anything less than removing work from their workload, it will be prone to failure. If RTIM appears like more work in addition to their current workload, they will not adopt it. No one needs another job on top of their existing job—your front line is no different.

Try to really understand their environment, their "What's In It For Me" (WIIFM), and then design a "smarter" end user experience. Do not just cram this new capability down your end users throat.

It is your responsibility to prioritize the interactions between your agents and between the people that they communicate with.

Business ROI Strategies

Good decisions at the right time in the right interaction almost always drive return on investment. As you planned this effort, you defined high level benefits that this effort would produce. Just like your personal life, investments with negative return are usually bad ideas in the long run. Investing in interactions that do not have enough ROI potential should be uncovered before you even think about proceeding to develop the interaction. Do the math and cut your losses early. The cost of rework will be exponentially higher if you go through the effort of building, testing, and deploying the interaction only to discover what you should have known initially: The interaction did not have enough business benefit to drive profit.

I know I have stated many times to start small, that is true, but make sure you start with an interaction that has enough business benefit to justify not only the initial investment but also creates enough benefit to pay for future efforts. When done correctly, I have seen these efforts essentially "print money" in the form of business benefit. If you take your eye off the ROI ball, it could be the beginning of the end before you even get out of the gate. You will need to link your business ROI strategies with operational decisions that are delivered through your decision management system. You should use these systems and business capabilities to achieve effective strategies and objectives to do with ROI.

The decisions that you make will impact your ROI over time. There are three main kinds of decisions, as I have discussed before: strategic, tactical, and operational.

1. Strategic decisions are few in number, large in impact.
2. Tactical decisions are for management and control and have a moderate impact.
3. Operational decisions are day-to-day decisions that affect one customer or transaction.

Decisions implement strategy and maximize customer value. If you prioritize your decisions correctly, you will be able to create a sustainable ROI for your business.

A structured ROI analysis improves business alignment between the core departments that have a stake in the interaction(s). In order to find out what the top tier results are, analysis like this should be carried out on an on-going basis.

These ROI analyses can either be done quickly or in a detailed manner so that comprehensive implementation plans are created as they are needed. The ultimate goal is to generate business value.

Even though business ROI strategies must be a priority, they need to be contemplated in parallel with customer and agent experience and interactions.

When customers, partners, and suppliers interact with your business, there needs to be an immediate contribution in every transaction. Being able to drive tangible business benefit as each customer interaction executes in the form of business transactions is the ideal ROI alignment, and the results will be incremental profit that will start to look like "free cash" to the business. Proving the linkage between individual transactions and incremental profit will be necessary to demonstrate success.

CHAPTER 8
Setting Business Expectations

"Being in control of your life and having realistic expectations about your day-to-day challenges are the keys to stress management, which is perhaps the most important ingredient to living a happy, healthy and rewarding life."

MARILU HENNER

In today's business, projects are investments of resource effort that a business allots for a need to be defined and justified in order to be accepted and implemented into your current business model. If you plan your work in a feasible way and execute that plan in an effective way, you can often accomplish what you set out to do. While this is not a book about project management approaches, it is about understanding that TIPP is about creating structure that drives change and that this happens through a semi-structured project management approach.

Developing the team charter and the initial plan is one such approach. Together with your multiple core leadership teams, you will outline your program and project management focus as it relates to your business and your goal of successfully implementing real time interaction management systems.

Program and Project Management 101

Defined, project management is simply the planning, organizing, securing, and managing of resources in order to bring about the successful completion of a predefined project. Decision management plays an important role in program and agile project management.

The business organization will have just as much, if not more, to do in designing interactions as the technology teams do. Do not underestimate the tasks that will need to be executed by the business! The steps will flow like this: Strategy (growth, cost reduction, customer experience), People (who is the customer, ROI, needs, service preferences, actions), The Interaction, People Interaction Execution (comp, training, performance, agent experience), Process (what business process is driving or impacting the interaction), Intelligence (what pieces of information do we need as the process executes), and Technology (what data do we need to create the insights/information that will be leveraged in the interaction).

Most successful companies have switched over to the agile project management method. It is applied to project management practice in software departments. If you can relate it to software, you can better understand how it works. This project management method should be used to enhance your results.

The Agile project management method is much more distinct than PMBOK or PRINCE2. It is highly flexible, which means that project deliverables can be altered without substantial changes. Big tasks are broken down into smaller tasks and stages that allow for significant risk reduction by using early assessment, testing, and analysis.

The Agile process involves setting a scope for every project, and it emphasizes that the whole team needs to work as an integrated unit. A few other factors of the Agile method are frequent communication, short-term delivery in cycles, and the setting of techniques and tools to implement the software accurately. I have personally seen this work from implementation to delivery.

Setting Your Business Scope

The scope of your business refers to everything that is required of you within the context of this project. Use TIPP when setting your scope—do not think of one particular area (technology or people for example); instead, think of them all holistically. Setting scope lends itself to expectation management. Small changes often result in massive obstacles that drive projects and programs to fail. You will be designing and implementing decision management systems so that your real time interactions are greatly improved.

This means that you will need a general outline of what you can expect to be working on from now until your system is functional. From there, it is a process of maintaining your decision management systems for increased ROI.

To set your business scope, you will first need to gain a firm grasp on each of your TIPP-approach elements. Technology, intelligence, process, and people will outline the scope of your business fairly well.

- ***Technology:*** This involves data, which is often the most expensive and longest scope to fulfill. Do not underestimate it. This involves creating and implementing business rules management systems, predictive analytics, optimization systems, decision management systems, and data infrastructure and the creation of a service-orientated platform within your business.
- ***Intelligence:*** The assembling of data to make information takes a fair amount of time. Often the biggest challenge for intelligence is understanding which question we are trying to build intelligence for. Make sure you allocate time to not only develop initial intelligence models but to provide sufficient time to test and refine intelligence.

- ***Process:*** This is not only designing the process but ensuring there is foundational support (people and technology) to execute the processes consistently. At this level, you will manage your decision inventory, adapt the software lifecycle, create decision service integration patterns, promote a culture of experimentation, and move over to fact-based decisions in business.
- ***People:*** This is about training, communication, and incentive alignment. Create and work with your three core departments—IT, analytics, and business—build a decision management center of excellence, and bring about clear organizational change.

When you set your business scope, remember that whenever you are charged with laying out the parameters and intentions of a project, you will encounter many obstacles. Part of defining the scope of a project is identifying and eliminating these obstacles.

During your predefined schedule, you will decide which features to include and which to leave out of your new systems. Scoping a project is really an engineering choice, where you have to position the project within an existing business. Using the Agile project management method, you can easily set the scope of your project before you begin.

In an Agile project, the entire team is responsible for management, not just the project manager. With procedures and processes, common sense is used over any written policies. This guarantees that there is no delay in management decision making—so things move forward faster.

The Agile method will also show you the leadership and skills of others and how motivating this can be for a team. The project manager here will simply facilitate and coordinate the processes, activities, and resources that the rest of the team will use during planning, building, and implementation.

For decision management and real time interaction

management systems, your company will want to consider using the Agile project management framework to help you outline and execute upon a business scope for your project.

Formally Establishing and Leveraging Interaction Ownership and Sponsorship

In your planning and preparation, you identified a senior member, ideally a C-level executive, that is potentially willing to "own" the interaction you are about to design as well as take controlled risks for major company gains. This leader should not be afraid to "sell" the vision to their peers and superiors. Because so many people will see this as a threat within your organization, you will need a business or operations leader that is not afraid to have those tough conversations.

Finding the right strategic target will be challenging. Just remember to always focus on how the key sponsor has been incentivized to perform and how it is measured by the business. Design interactions to move those key metrics, and you will find yourself in a great place more often. Technology is not the right function to own these efforts for long periods of time, as it really needs to be owned by the business.

It is normal for technology to be a key partner on this journey. However, for it to be successful, the business must be accountable for the interactions, and that includes the direction provided throughout the design process.

The owner does not always have to be the key sponsor. Sometimes executives will sponsor upstream efforts in order to ease their business pain, and the upstream organization will actually own the interaction. For example, a credit or collection agency "sponsors" a financial risk management system to ensure new customers pay the same deposit amounts for services across all customer facing channels, regardless of the system used to inquire for the service.

The deposit amount and processes associated with the

interaction are consistent, despite how the customer interacts with your business. The channel's owners (especially the sales organization in this case) must have "skin in the game" to ensure that interaction are accurately executed.

As you design interaction, you will soon discover that there is some creativity in how a business must balance its need to survive with its willingness to change and adapt. The capability is going to test that balance. A strong leader with solid partnerships and execution channel leaders will prove to be critical. With most technology, organizations are focused and fueled by capital dollars, so you need a leader that can make the organization a reality within the business operations process.

An executive sponsor—also called a project sponsor—is a role in project management taken up by the most senior member, the chair or a top member on the project board. Establishing who will be your project sponsor is key because they will be responsible for the success of implementing your new real time interaction management systems.

Establishing ownership of this new project means collecting the people together that will assist in making it a company-wide triumph. That means bringing the stakeholder groups of people together that have a vested interest in the effort being successful. Your business department(s) and analytics and IT departments need to work together as one coherent unit.

Effective business impact depends on your ability to establish applicable business benefits that you can translate into specific business rules. You will need design transparency, execution transparency, collaboration, impact analysis, and a platform for analytics if you want provide the transparency into the process as well as uncover new opportunities—an output of analytics. It will take partnership across teams and business functions to effectively create and implement these systems.

Companies need to accept accountability for their front-line decisions while working to make them more effective in this highly competitive global marketplace. Before you can put together the "what" and "how," you need to find the appropriate "who." This means establishing both ownership and sponsorship for your project.

- You need to find key members of your team structure that will offer expertise, knowledge, and support during the execution of these key decision management steps. IT, analytics, and business teams will be involved in the selection.
- You will also need to seek out an executive sponsor to oversee the success of your project from beginning to end. They will need to be involved just like everyone else, and they will accept responsibility if the implementation phase fails.

Your executive sponsor will be the person you see to secure the right project resources, build management support, and provide the correct funding to the team. They set expectations, review key deliverables, and eliminate obstacles that are identified during the process. They sell the vision and concept to all levels of the organization.

Timing, Resources, and Scheduling

Because ownership of the project lies with many different parties, namely the project team, the stakeholders, and the other employees, there is a need for the executive sponsor to help drive everyone from the individual departments to come up with a functional timeline and a detailed list of the resources they will need throughout the project.

While executive sponsors are very important during the start-up and design phases of the project, they allow the team a lot of leeway, and while they remain engaged with the team during implementation, they also allow them to do their jobs. The executive sponsor is the highest ranking team member, but there are still project managers and team leaders.

A workable timeline will need to be established based on input from all the key players in all departments. Then, preferably using the Agile project management methodology, schedule times will be set. Of course, before this can be done, the correct resources need to be discussed, sourced, and delivered—or the project cannot begin.

Once the initial business case has been developed and the right executive sponsor identified, project initiation has begun. Then team selection and establishment can take place. The teams will need to be briefed and commissioned. A communication plan will have to be created to reinforce collaboration.

Then comes the project initiation, requirements, and design phases, where the "steering" group will be validated, the root causes of issues discussed, and process mapping will occur. Interactions will be designed from the outside in; roles, metrics, and organizational design will be evaluated.

IT implications will be discussed, transition plans will be created, and the business case will be progressed. The final three phases are development, implementation, and results or maintenance. Everything requires a schedule, the correct timelines, and efficient planning for adequate ordering and usage of resources.

Above all, your business scope has got to suit your timelines and existing budget. Your organization will only have a certain amount of budgetary and human resources to dedicate to a project of this magnitude. You have to try and make this complex implementation work within these predefined limitations. It is also why choosing the right sponsor is important.

Once you have successfully plotted your route forward with your project team, you can begin creating interactions that you want to use in your new real time interaction management systems. It is going to be a challenge to get it right, but it will change the way you do business forever.

CHAPTER 9

Creating Interactions That Align Strategy to Technology

> *"There's an old joke among software developers. When something works in an unexpected but strangely effective way, the developers often kid, 'Oh, that's not a bug. That's a feature.' While this is usually a joke, designers can use the same technique of reframing the problem when tackling their own projects. In fact, there's an old joke among designers: 'It's not a problem. It's an opportunity.'"*
>
> DAN SAFFER

How do you create interactions that align strategic real time interaction management to technology? The simple answer is to know what your options are and to have a team of people with the right expertise to help you make the best decision.

It begins with assessing your business capabilities and then asking whether you should build or buy the supporting technology system. Your data design needs to create the information that you will use to implement strategic interactions between your business and your customer.

How to Assess Business Capabilities in Terms of Technology

All businesses begin with limited resources and budgets, which is why it is crucial to assess the phase of business mapping that involves using fact-based methods for determining where to invest these finite resources.

Assessing your business capability in terms of technology means that you will be looking at different perspectives and weighing up how these perspectives contribute to business importance and performance. When you adequately assess your technological business capabilities, you will benefit in many far-reaching ways.

A fact-based method will help you identify strengths and weaknesses, plus you will be able to see how your existing capabilities limit your organization's ability to achieve your new business goals. You know that you need to assess your technological infrastructure and results. To do this, follow these simple steps:

- Create a standard unit of measurement. Every team member in your project management team will complete an assessment and will score their answers using this set unit of measurement. A three- or five-point scale will do.
- Use a hybrid scale approach. Do a broad assessment of all business capabilities within your current scope. Once this has been done, look deeper into the capabilities that you have deemed "the most important."
- Once your high-level assessment is done, look at the areas that concern you the most. You should have a list of areas like "difficult to use, frequent errors.'" Record the scaled answers in a report and calculate the capability's overall performance.
- Get your team to answer the assessments. You will have a range of opinions from three of your top departments giving you a broader spectrum view of the things you need to improve, add, remove, or completely change.

To Buy or to Build?

When it comes to information technology and strategy, there is always one question that your team will have to face during the capabilities assessment. Do we build our own system, or do we buy an existing system? The answer is totally subjective and will depend on your business requirements and long-term needs.

Some experts say that it is a waste of time building new systems when technology is updated so often. Others say that building a system gives you greater control over functionality as it pertains to your business in particular. Perspective will certainly play a role in your decision.

There are criteria that you can use to determine whether your business should build or buy their own information systems. These are core vs. context, timing, coverage, scale, standards, direction, and TCO.

- *Core vs. context:* Determine whether your information systems will affect the core of your business. Few organizations would worry about custom building a system for something general like payroll or supply chain management, but put the system in the right CONTEXT, and you may find that a custom system is more beneficial.
- *Timing:* While buying is certainly quicker than creating a custom solution, it is not the only reason to choose a bought solution. Typically, installing, configuring, customizing, and completing data conversions are just as timely as custom development. You will need a much better reason to buy, than "It's quicker."
- *Coverage:* Does the bought solution match what the business requires vs. what the package solution provides? Test the coverage of these "paid" solutions. At least 80% of what you require should be offered by these brands, or there is no point buying it. Determine what they offer, what they do not

offer, and which features you could use in the future as you grow and progress.

- **Scale:** If the system is large, it really needs to support your core business functions. Scale is essential when you begin measuring and mitigating risk for your project. Compare costs and risk before you decide on the size of your system.
- **Standards:** Perhaps the most important of all the criteria are the standards that your system will possess. Much of your system needs to be consistent in order for it to genuinely reduce the costs of development by spreading it over a larger community over time.
- **Direction:** When you think about purchasing a standard solution, you need to consider how flexible, extensible, and maintainable it will be and for how long. Systems generally need to last a long time, so direction is vital in continued growth. Your company should be able to add new features with little trouble.
- **TCO:** Total cost of ownership includes the cost of acquisition, configuration, customization, support, maintenance, and growth of the information system that you either buy or build. You do not want to pay for services you do not need.

In-House vs. Vendor Resources–Guidelines for Successful Establishment

Whether you decide to choose in-house building or vendor resources to have your real time interaction management systems created, you will need some guidelines for successful establishment. There are pros and cons for each type that I discuss briefly here.

In-house Build

- Establish the business rules that you will need to make your project a success.

- Be prepared to bypass the business rules that are not applicable.
- Use patterns to inform your decision making system process
- Use all three groups—IT, analytics, and business teams—in the evaluation and decision process.
- All platforms should contain design transparency, execution transparency, collaboration, impact analysis, and analytics.
- Create a sustainable business rules management system.
- Focus on analytic decisions—predicting risk, fraud, and opportunity.
- Create decision services that work with business rules, optimization, and predictive analytics.
- Begin with the decision in mind, be transparent and agile, be predictive not reactive and test, learn, and continually improve.

PROS: Create a system you need, save on unnecessary costs, get local support, no obsolescence, you control all investments and enhancements, and it gives you an advantage

CONS: Any solution changes can be costly, upfront costs, risk of losing knowledge base, no economies of scale, and trouble supporting new technology platforms over time

Vendor Resources

- Find a vendor that has your best interests at heart and an excellent track record with their support and maintenance services.
- Establish top level objectives and strategies before handing over the project.
- Executive and cross functional teams must visit the vendor, if the budget allows. Face to face meetings tend to keep things moving along smoothly.

- Be sure to get commercial approval on every step or at every phase of the project lifecycle.

PROS: The majority of your needs are met instantly; there is fast deployment; all design, development, and testing is handled; and the knowledge base is spread out over many resources.

CONS: There is a high chance that features are missing, not all enhancements are relevant to your business, and the vendor may not know your business.

The question of whether to go with an in-house team or a vendor resource is something that needs to be discussed and decided by your whole team, including your sponsor. Then you will need to sit down and thresh out the guidelines that you will use for successful establishment of each process.

Designing Data to Create Information

If you are going to align strategy with technology, you will need to consider how data is represented so that it can be used efficiently by the people that matter. Technology collects and captures information, but it can also be configured to display this information in easy-to-consume ways.

The first part of designing applicable data first comes down to the business question you are trying to answer. For instance, let's look at a few examples:

For a growth strategy, the question may be: What is this customer most likely to buy from me? For a retention strategy, the question might be: Does this customer want to leave me? For a customer experience strategy, the question might be: What type of customer experience has this customer had, and do I need to intervene?

When you do design data, make sure it is supporting "actionable" intelligence. We will talk more about that when we link intelligence to RTIM.

As far as data, you would design the data you need to support a system that answers the business question for every applicable customer. That means you design the data in a way that will feed the predictive model and/or business rules, which will in turn feed the business process. There have been many advances recently in data technology that help you do some of this data design work, but in the end, it will come down to someone making the decision as to what data will be needed to support answering the business question that is embedded in the business process.

Designers create data visualizations in the form of graphs, charts, and using color in interesting ways. What happens if you have thousands, even millions, of pieces of data that need to be represented in a legible way?

Instead of seeing your customer profiles in black and white, you will need to build a data foundation that allows your business to see each individual customer in color. Then you can use these excellent colors to review their history and context so that the next best action can be taken for sales and/or other business opportunities.

The way data is designed affects the outcome of your processes and strategies. Using a predictive analysis, decision management, and guided interactions system, data suddenly becomes one of the most important factors when reviewing the needs for the interaction.

Data is the foundation of the interaction. It is the first thing you should think about in the TIPP process as you design your first interaction. Data is the focus here, and you need to make sure that when you design, data is usually the "long pole in the tent." It costs the most to get from technology and usually takes the longest to validate and implement. Data availability and quality is critical to system performance. Before you even consider buying a piece of technology, spend ample time thinking about the customer and about operational and competitive information that you will need for your first interaction.

Design the system around the data platform that you intend to use as the performance and speed of the interaction will be critical for long-term success. Think about your real interactions—pauses and miscues impact the conversation with real interactions and not in a favorable way. This is what happens if data availability and system performance are not contemplated as you begin to design your interactions.

Do not forget the data GIGO (garbage in garbage out). Understanding the timing of data availability is important—in hours, days—how old the data is will certainly impact its effectiveness in some cases. Poor system performance will stifle end-user adoption and ultimately risk your investment. The same goes if end-users are getting bad information or intelligence as a result of bad data.

This is something to think about now, before you begin actually designing your data systems. Any piece of technology can gather data, but it takes a really well designed system to represent it in a useable way.

You need to think about the people that will be reviewing this information, the point in the interaction / time they will need the information, and how much easier it will be for them if the data is designed correctly. This is how you plan for future success with your real time interaction management systems.

Strategic Interactions for RTIM

When it comes to strategy linkage, we discussed in the planning phase that there are multiple strategies that can be chosen when it comes to RTIM. If you recall, we discussed that strategy can be grouped into three primary buckets:

- *Growth* – Your strategy should create more growth and opportunity for the company. This could be measured by things like: more revenue, more revenue per transaction, incremental revenue perhaps from a new product or service, etc.
- *Customer Experience* – Increasing the experience for customers has far reaching impacts for the business. Typically, it is an

indicator of loyalty and has huge churn reduction capability. This strategy could be measured by things like: NPS scores at a transaction as well as a brand level, churn reduction, etc.
- *Cost Reduction* – This strategy is more about eliminating operational costs, perhaps with a specific product or service or with a certain segment of customers. This can measured by things like: cost to serve, avoidable cost per transaction, AHT (in call center environments), etc.

A strategic interaction involves the process of getting several parties aligned to achieve a common goal. It usually takes some serious communication and motivation for these people to move forward and pursue that goal. In real time interaction management, your long-term strategy should be to have your strategic interactions implemented on a company-wide basis. That means enterprise wide and every applicable contact channel running through one centralized system. Every part of the interaction feeds directly back to the business conductors. It is a whole new level of business control that you will need to prepare the business for.

For integration into human contact channels, all front-end staff and applicable call center agents will need to be briefed on how your systems work, as well as how they are going to be integrated into their applicable business processes.

You will always need clear and concise communication to achieve viable strategic interactions with your customer base. Before you launch into creating a real time interaction management system, you need to know which strategic interactions are the most important and how your company can use them within this system context.

Remember that every interaction with customers tells them something about your business—how much they are valued or not valued. Interactions prove to customers that brand promises are either real or fake. You need to figure out what you want your customers to think, feel, and do at every stage of the relationship as you design the interaction.

This is how you create effective strategic interactions. All of your business processes should enable brand promises to be realized through strategic customer experiences. From answering the phone, to replying to an email, to retweeting or dealing with someone in person—all interactions should be strategic.

Otherwise, how will your company ever learn to optimize them using predictive analytics and decision management? Strategic interactions for real time interaction management systems need be thought out, designed, and tested very carefully. You need to know what your system is going to DO and how it will make your customers FEEL.

Take the emotional, intellectual, and behavioral state of the customer into account. Feeling, thinking, and doing are what make up the interactions that we have. In order to harness these for greater sales, your system will need to fully understand these interactions and how to transform them into strategic interactions with end goals.

CHAPTER 10

Creating Interactions That Align Intelligence to RTIM

> *"Don't bury logic in channel applications. The decisioning engine is the brain, the channel application is the delivery mechanism."*
>
> SURESH VITTAL

If you are going to improve customer interactions one decision at a time, you will need to know how to align business intelligence to this goal. It is your job to use the business intelligence that your company has gathered and analyzed to support your overall objectives for your real time interaction management systems.

That means investigating and aligning the right kinds of business intelligence to these real time systems to create interactions for your customers that steadily improve profit over time. To begin, you need to know which questions to ask in relation to your core intelligence strategies.

Questions on Channels, Targets, and Tactics

Every customer uses certain contact channels or devices when interacting with your brand. Real time interaction management systems use all available information about that customer to predict or determine what future action, offer, content, or discount to present them. In this way, each customer is TARGETED via a certain CHANNEL based on a strategy-driven TACTIC designed to contribute to a strategic business objective, and it is delivered to the interaction by an RTIM system.

The business intelligence collected from each customer and the predictive models that are leveraged or developed will drive and support these customer interactions. That is why you need to carefully select which pieces of data will be most effective for the automated predictive analytics model and which decisions will result in a successful interaction that will in turn drive the desired customer experience.

Your organization will need to ask itself questions about your marketing channels, your individual customer targets, and the tactics that you will use to interact with these customers. It may become apparent that traditional marketing channels that focus primarily on sales may need to be leveraged for non-sales activity. For example, instead of directly approaching a customer with an offer, it might be better for the business and the customer to not try to sell more product or service and choose instead to approach them with a survey, an event, or a loyalty reward depending on the supporting channel and customer intelligence. Your business needs to agree to the concept of non-sales activity on traditional sales channels before you start building the supporting systems that can drive those kinds of interactions.

- Questions on marketing or delivery channels must be addressed.
- Questions on customer targets should be addressed.

- Questions on strategy and supporting business intelligence tactics must be addressed.

Everything from the selection of the marketing channel, to the decided-upon intended result and ROI, to the tactic used must be discussed and organized by your project management team. Your organization may have thousands or even millions of interactions with customers during the course of a day. Your job is to ensure that these interactions are being guided by the right business intelligence.

Real time business intelligence will give your company tactical support at the transaction level when driving company strategies that are shaped by real time events. Transactions now become strategic in outcome because they were designed that way intentionally. When you get the process and intelligence integration correct, you will know because the tangible benefits will start to flow back to the business, and customer experiences and other key measures will start flowing in the direction in which you intended—whether that is customer conversion, retention, improved experiences, whatever it may be.

Design Your Opportunities

A real time business intelligence system is also called an event-driven system. These systems must react to events as they happen to get the most out of customer experiences and other opportunities.

With these systems you will be able to "react" with intelligence to events as they happen. Because this capability can be a double edged sword, your real time business intelligence technology will need to be designed to reduce risk and automatically identify opportunities as they arise.

You will be able to profit from immediate, actionable decisions before the opportunity with a particular customer vanishes.

Using your business intelligence—that is, using data, trend and pattern detection, and predictive models—actionable insight is immediately returned to your employee or decision-maker, which enables them to take advantage of an opportunity with a high degree of confidence.

- To adequately design your opportunities, you need to figure out how to use your organization's disparate data to provide meaningful information and analyses to people in your company that are in charge of decision-making.

They will then seize this information and transform it into actionable strategy, which will result in increased efficiency, cost reduction, customer retention, and sales improvements.

Imagine using real time business intelligence in retail to improve sales patterns. Based on how your system has been set up and programmed and the decisions that have been made to accompany these systems, you will be able to see—automatically—that the customer standing in front of your front-end sales person always buys products with free gifts.

In an instant, the system could relay this information to your sales person, who will then upsell products that contain free gifts. The chances are that this will result in improved sales as that customer leaves with more products than they intended to buy. Designing an opportunity like this all relies on how effectively your business intelligence system is designed to work.

If your staff, partners, suppliers, and decision-makers are supplied with the right information, in the right format, concerning the right people, at the right time—opportunities can always be leveraged.

Creating and Leveraging Information

For a very long time, to optimize the decision cycle, you had to compress or shorten it. The best business intelligence money could buy was found in data warehouses and marts that were updated overnight with data from legacy operational systems. But because of the need for real time solutions to reduce time latency, better solutions were created.

Real time data collection, analysis, and decision-making are now crucial to the business intelligence environment. Immediate decisions that are made in real time according to collected data is where you want your business intelligence to be.

Strategic business intelligence focuses on achieving the long-term goals of an organization. Tactical business intelligence focuses on short-term organizational goals—like a specific transaction or marketing tactic. These days, operational business intelligence seeks to optimize a wider range of decisions by integrating business operations with intelligence.

It is true that right time business intelligence reduces latency and time to take action, which in turn increases business value. Creating and leveraging information for your business intelligence systems means defining the scope for your strategic, tactical, and operational needs. Putting together an adequate business intelligence strategy that is properly in line with your business goals is not an easy process.

On the whole, business intelligence needs to include processes, technologies, and stakeholders that can effectively gather, integrate, access, and analyze information so that your company can make better decisions over time. You will need to take into account the right framework, methodology, process, governance, system, and technology to get your business intelligence systems delivering enough value that aligns with your business goals.

Business intelligence needs to follow a set cycle if it has to work well. From decisions and actions, vision and strategy, business drivers, business planning, business process, and organization, to governance, data architecture, and technology—these are all steps in that information creation cycle.

- Always create a business case and detail the benefits.
- Get your buy-in from senior executives or sponsors.

- Always use an enterprise-wide perspective.
- Detail the criteria you will need for success.
- Always use best practices and implement change management procedures.
- Business intelligence must align with your business process and your IT capabilities.
- Always work with frameworks and proven methods.
- Consider all components of business intelligence.

Once you have completed the assessments of process, technology, intelligence, and people using the TIPP approach, then you can begin building your real time interaction management systems. Current state vs. intended state matters when you are about to implement such radical and new structures into your business.

Customer Insights

Customer insights are part of your business intelligence solution that helps your organization keep time, cost, and risks low while improving overall sales.

Take a fashion house for example. If the company instantly knew what each customer's style preferences were based on a buying persona, this could be communicated to the front-end sales assistant, who would then implement quality sales processes to upsell or cross sell in-store products to a specific customer. This sort of data cannot be found from transactions alone.

In fact, you need customer insights to complete the information gathering process. By combining customer insights with real time business intelligence, you will understand what motivates certain customers to buy. Then you can compare buying behavior from researched customer insights done on a face-to-face basis.

When you combine these two elements, you get a more complete picture of your customer behavior. It moves you from the "what" to the "why." Then you will be able to customize and personalize your customer's purchasing experience—just because you added insight to your existing data. You can then test your assumptions about customers and optimize them.

If you want your business to be a customer intelligent business (and you do), then applied customer insight is the most direct route. With applied customer insight, it is not only face-to-face interactions we are talking about. There are also social interactions online and dozens of other places where your customers openly engage with your brand.

If you can leverage these opportunities, then you can guarantee that your marketing strategies and IT infrastructures work together towards your business goals. You can often purchase or build an ACI (applied customer insights) solution that is made up of customer analytics, customer intelligent organization, and customer management solutions.

The goal is to capture, interpret, and act on these insights as quickly as possible. For example, a multichannel campaign will improve the customer experience due to engagement. Data will be pulled in from direct marketing, email, websites, business applications, social media, mobile, transactional systems, and more.

This data will be augmented and transformed into customer insights. These insights can include predictive analytics, market information, real time mobile information or social networking, web analytics, segmentation, and more. You will nurture social communities to achieve this insight and deliver a quality customer experience.

With the right intelligence, a large computer manufacturer can perform the following functions: A customer calls into your service center to get their computer repaired. After the tech resolves the problem, the system would recommend add-ons based specifically on the model in the interaction. The customer expresses interest but is not able to make a decision at that moment.

The customer never calls the call center back. A month later that same customer visits the company's website. The first thing they are shown is the offer or item previously discussed; it is completely tailor-made for that individual. Will the customer buy it then? The chances are so much higher than before. This is a simple example of creating intelligent interactions across business channels and business functions.

The data will be interpreted by analytic teams, research and development teams, supply chain partners, sales and marketing teams, operations, manufacturing, and more. When marketing and IT collaborate, effective customer insights are added to the business intelligence pool, streamlining the information received.

When you are able to synthesize all available data, internally and externally, to produce a unified view of the business that is accessible by all who work there, effective decisions will be made. Your business intelligence strategy needs to be agile and adaptive. It is constantly evolving to meet the needs of your business in a demanding market.

CHAPTER 11
Creating Interactions That Align People to RTIM

"No institution can possibly survive if it needs geniuses or supermen to manage it. It must be organized in such a way as to be able to get along under a leadership composed of average human beings."

PETER DRUCKER

If you are going to successfully align people to real time interaction management, then you need to get a firm grasp on what motivates people. This means considering behavior drivers like incentives, training, the agent's environment, and how people within your company communicate as well as how often.

Creating interactions is difficult enough, but when you have to align these interactions with the goals that your people have set for your real time interaction management systems, the challenge increases. Let's look at some different assessments you can conduct to get you thinking about your employee performance.

Incentive Assessment

Incentives and compensation are commonly used to align people in your business with the organization's core goals. Things like revenue increases, customer experience improvement, customer retention, and conversion are all goals that the CEO and board of directors are looking for when they make investments in the business, and that is also what they plan on achieving with any new system implementation.

In order to stay on track, you need to be prepared to conduct an incentive assessment to see who in your leadership hierarchy should be financially motivated to make this effort succeed.

An incentive assessment is tied to ownership and leadership in a company as well as desired behavior you are looking for to be exhibited. Here are some questions you should ask and some things you should determine when performing your next incentive assessment:

- How am I going to structure my incentive program to effectively motivate members in my cross functional teams to execute the intended interaction?
- How will my top tier incentives differ from my group incentives for executing this interaction?
- How am I going to structure my incentive program for my sponsors? (senior executive in charge)
- Which incentive structures will I consider for cross-functional teams in general to ensure this interaction gets executed?
- Determine the evaluation criteria to determine effectiveness for your various incentive systems.
- Determine who the reward recipients will be and when it is appropriate to award these incentives.
- Determine what reward type you will offer (cash, vacation, prizes, time off).

Training Needs Assessment

The people in your company do not just step into new system positions and know what to do. They will require full and extensive training as well as experience to be good at what they are doing.

A training needs assessment is conducted to determine the performance requirements, skills, knowledge, and abilities needed by your cross functional team. This will help you choose your team members more accurately as you will have to invest in people that are willing to drive this new discipline forward, not the organization.

Hopefully, if the training needs assessment is done well, the right amount of resources will be dedicated to the people that need them most. There are usually three levels in a basic training needs assessment. These can be adapted according to the requirements of your company.

1. *Individual assessment:* In this section, you will analyze how well an individual employee does their job. Then you will judge their capacity for taking on the new work of executing these interactions. Things like stress levels, workload, environment complexity, work ethic,, and competency are taken into account.
2. *Organizational assessment:* This section evaluates the level of organizational performance. It will determine what sort of skills, abilities, and knowledge is needed for executing this particular interaction.
3. *Occupational assessment:* In this section, you will identify which occupational discrepancies exist that will be introduced by the interactions.

The steps in a training needs assessment are straightforward, and your company probably already has a system outlined for this eventuality. You will move from identifying potential team candidates to planning the training administration and conducting them in a safe and secure environment.

Make sure that every member of your cross functional team goes through this process. It will help them identify the nature of their future work and will begin the re-alignment process that must happen in order to successfully execute a system of this magnitude.

Current Rep Environment Assessment

You will need to assess your rep's current environment. This means taking note of things like access to information, types of information, effectiveness of information, tools to perform their job, performance of these tools, delivery of tools/information, and integrated desktop, or many tools with scattered awareness and usage.

Put yourself in the end user's shoes. When you properly design your solution, it should make the agent's experience better. Make it worse and you will risk your investment. To do this, you must physically shadow your agents to understand their challenges. Listen to the interactions they handle. What is it like? Is it managed chaos, is it scripted, or is it somewhere in the middle? Think about performing in their place as you design the interaction. If you would not do what you are asking them to do, you can safely assume that they will care even less than you do about implementing your new interactions.

To align your team members with your business goals, you will have to conduct a specific environmental assessment to determine the current representative state of your business environment as it pertains to the front-line people that work there.

This assessment is carried out by your sponsor or another key team member and involves the process of estimating and evaluating the short- and long-term effects of these new real time interaction management systems on the quality of your agent's environment.

- Detail who will be involved in the environmental testing phase.
- Plan the scope of the assessment by including key members of your project management teams.
- Conduct the assessment, keeping in mind that it is only representative of the business environment over a specific time.
- Analyze and assemble reports based on the assessment findings.
- Review the initial environmental assessment to determine what the positive and negative impacts of real time interaction management may be on your staff.
- Make the necessary decisions based on your report conclusions.
- Take action to mitigate the negative impact of your new systems.
- Follow up by conducting a similar test a few months after system launch and implementation.

Keep in mind that an environmental assessment is only a version of the truth and takes factors into account like date, time, people involved, and the leadership that was conducting the assessments in the first place. What you are looking for is a clear path in your business environment, where your people will successfully align RTIM with your business goals.

Communication Channels and Frequency

If you are going to align your people with the goals for your business, you need to understand the communication channels that you will be using to communicate with the people who will be executing your interactions.

This is about organizational communication at all levels, from the leadership to the front line. How will you identify people who need to receive status and updates and the timing of these messages? Does the front line respond to email? How does your leadership team want to be communicated with? In person, via email, or on Skype, and how often is it possible to do this?

Designing interactions that you plan to integrate into your business is challenging enough. The point of this chapter is to make sure the people within your organization are communicated to and, more importantly, that you communicate to them in an effective way down an effective channel. Events and changes can happen quickly when building and running these systems; communication will be critical especially when you have to change course, so make sure you know how to effectively reach your people along the journey.

CHAPTER 12

Creating Interactions That Align Process to RTIM

"Organizations with cultures that value continuous improvement are far better at changing their processes and staying competitive. Yet most organizations that make a run at continuous improvement fail to make it stick because of fear."

BRAD POWER

The truth is that nearly all business process management programs that are not aligned with your business strategy fail miserably. The leadership of your business needs to approve and commit to your program before it is implemented. The team must be held accountable for delivering quality processes that are aligned with your organizational goals.

When I talk about process, it is important to understand that when I say "implement" a process, this statement assumes that the organizational support will be implemented to sustain the new process and interactions. Business architecture activities are critical to success. Planning the resources that you will need to successfully implement these interactions is necessary for positive results to materialize.

Your business relies on the long-term repeat business of your customers. That is why your business process management program needs to deliver better customer outcomes and experiences at a much lower cost than your competitors. This must be sustainable, and when done correctly, it will bring about complete organizational transformation.

Intelligent Business Process

Your company will need a new framework for creating intelligent business processes that are aligned with your business goals. There are many methodologies available to use in today's world: Lean, Lean Six Sigma, and Agile to name a few core methods.

Six Sigma is a type of approach used to identify key process characteristics that matter to your customer. It discovers the process inputs that influence these characteristics and then implements improvements to impress the customer.

At its core is the fundamental need for continuous improvement, a philosophy that characterizes the Six Sigma approach. Using the right software, you can implement Six Sigma into your intelligent business processes. You will be able to manage your controls dynamically and in real time.

You need to model and automate your business rules and processes. Then historical process data can be reviewed, and real time processes can be adjusted and improved as the need arises. With Six Sigma tools and real time management of your business processes, you can leverage many process capabilities, like process specialization, monitoring, rule definition, situation selection, and execution.

This works together to result in event correlation and eventual continuous improvement, which is a key component of all effective intelligent business process frameworks. The steps involved with planning a Six Sigma intelligent business process is called a DMAIC methodology or approach.

They each stand for Define, Measure, Analyze, Improve, and Control. Critical information is captured, and performance targets are established. You will also be able to experiment with multiple versions of a single process to optimize it. Process controls are put in place to alert you to any violation of flow, value, or rules.

Six Sigma may or may not fit with your process monitoring methodology. I have used it many times and have found the methodology to be very effective in supporting the linkage of intelligence to business process.

Understanding Differentiated Service Treatment

When you attempt to treat one group or segment of customers differently than another, you are applying different "treatments" to one vs. another. By applying this to the service that you provide, you are executing "differentiated service treatment." For example, a loyalty program like Delta Airlines uses tiers to represent customer value: Diamond, Platinum, Gold, and Silver. These tiers of value are based and many variables about the specific customer. With customers being segmented by value, Delta can then offer different processes and service experiences based on the customer.

Now this is a neat service differentiator for Delta, and many customers who climb the tiers are much more loyal and will fly Delta first, often never considering a competitor. This is a great example of win-win; the customer gets a different service experience that generates loyalty, but the real power is what Delta can then do with this new transparency. By understanding the ROI for each group of customers, Delta can appropriately forecast and invest its operational budgets much more efficiently to provide the greatest benefit to the best customers. It may not sound like much, but when you can shave small percentages off of operational budgets, the real dollars behind these small percentages are multi-millions, sometimes billions, in savings.

Every customer gets a specific treatment from Delta, and these are different service experiences that you get because of your "status." When you design an interaction that treats one group differently than the other, you will exponentially have more scope to address to build, design, and test the interaction—and hence more work to do to ensure that each group gets the right treatments at the time of the correct interaction. Be careful when tackling a complex differentiated interaction. The testing strategy and execution will be critical in your success as the complexity for each dimension will be significant. One practice that works very well is to lay out a map of the interaction journey for each dimension of TIPP; do not forget to apply the journey map for each group that you want to treat that could be in that specific interaction.

Now, a differentiated service experience can help your organization build loyal customer bases as it has for Delta.

When customer experience better matches customer value, a successful differentiated service experience has occurred. Preferential treatment for certain customers is not a bad thing. That is why it is important that you consider implementing a differentiated service model when the ROI makes sense—as 90%[12] of surveyed customers say they would prefer it or they do not mind it.

It has been proven that when a company offers differentiated service to its customers, it improves brand perception. Customer satisfaction starts with the trust they instill in your brand. If your customers lose trust, they will move to another provider. The only way your organization can build trust is through collaboration, competence, reputation, and familiarity.

In other words, this is established partly through service delivery and partly through expectation setting. Many companies pour all of their focus into service delivery and none into expectation setting. But if you do not take charge of what your customer

---

12 Building a Differentiated Service Experience Strategy, Accenture, http://www.accenture.com/SiteCollectionDocuments/PDF/Accenture-Building-Differentiated-Service-Experience-Strategy.pdf

expects from you (based on your promises), it becomes impossible to achieve your targets.

It is up to you to proactively establish customer service expectations for your organization.

By agreeing to set service expectations with your customers by offering them differentiated service treatments, you can change customer perception about your organization and define a clear performance target for service delivery. Different clients require different levels of customer support, so support packages based on the particular customer should be offered at the time of purchase.

Customer experience transformation that begins with differentiated service treatments is first simple and easy with the goal of driving to detailed and sophisticated. You will need a deep understanding of customer segments, including insights and testing. The value your customer places on control and choice is also an important predictor of service-based behaviors and expectations.

Your organization needs to constantly deliver great customer experiences so that your processes are aligned with your ultimate service goals. This is how you will achieve financial success—by differentiating your service experiences when the return on investment will allow. This will in turn allow you to reinvest profitable dollars into additional efforts. It is almost like printing free money.

Future Processes

With the right business process framework, you can develop road maps, requirements, development plans, requirement gathering, and project methodologies to help you implement a Six Sigma-like system. A team charter will focus on the scope of a project. But the next phase is to create a workable process map.

You need to define a number of things if you are going to settle on the future processes of your business. These will include the process customer, which products and services are delivered to your customer that are vital to the business scope, the key processes that deliver these products, which inputs (human skills) are provided to the process, and who the supplier of the input is.

At this point, your business process must be imported into the right software so that you can see, via graphic representation, a detailed diagram of the steps that exist in your chosen process. Software can be created or bought to complete this need.

A good example is of a process map for an invoice application. Visually, the diagram will show you what happens once the invoice has been generated. Everything that comes after that is a process—from requesting additional information to approval of the invoice by the manager, rejection, sending the invoice, invoice delivery via mail, and all the steps that occur leading up to confirmation of payment.

When you use a software program like Visio within the program you have bought or created, it comes with a number of significant benefits. Real time process maps can be made available instantly without any need for additional research. There is flexibility in the level of detail used, and extras can be added to the process map over time.

The process map should support live production processes, which means that large, highly-detailed maps are needed and easily created using this software. More information is available regarding systems and actors than your typical process map. Finally, process characteristics like insights, service-level performance, and process participants are included.

The future processes of your business will be mapped out like this using advanced software and process mapping. They go a long way to ensuring that your intelligent business processes are completely aligned with your IT infrastructure, analytics, and differentiated service treatment.

With the rise of the importance of service level performance, the more streamlined, agile, and adaptive a business process is, the better. These maps can be automatically improved or manually updated according to your findings.

PART IV
TIPP Taking Action: Implementation of RTIM

CHAPTER 13
Strategy and Technology: Implementing Interactions

> *"The first rule of any technology used in a business is that automation applied to an efficient operation will magnify the efficiency. The second is that automation applied to an inefficient operation will magnify the inefficiency."*
>
> BILL GATES

To properly implement the technology involved with real time interaction management, it means that you need be aware of the options available to you in-house. There, you will be able to build a system that uses fast, real time technology to create a valuable, personalized experience for individual customers by tapping into big data.

Your project teams will build your real time interaction management system using the TIPP approach—with a focus on the four pillars of real time interaction: technology, intelligence, people, and process. If you get each segment right, soon your customer interactions will be driving with your business goals and earning you more incremental profit.

Building and Deploying Technology

Choosing to build and deploy your RTIM technology in-house is a great way to guarantee that it suits your business, is scalable, and is easy to update. However, we do not suggest this route unless you are a software company that is capable of building and maintaining these types of platforms. There are so many new providers that are making great strides in this category. There are so many risks with this type of technology development that it almost always makes sense to purchase from a leading provider.

It is a good idea to do some research first to see what your competition is using and how it has been working for them thus far. Forrester and Gartner are excellent research firms that provide intelligence and research around software providers in your industry's space. Once you have gauged what you are up against, you can take the plans you have created and begin your RTIM build.

- *Software & hardware for business rules management systems:* This includes components for creating, testing, managing, deploying, and maintaining business rules, or rule engines. This technology drives decision services forward.
- *Software & hardware for predictive analytics systems*: These are software components that are designed to enable the analysis of a set of data sources in order to determine the mathematical relationship in that data for predictive analytics models.
- *Software & hardware for Business Process Management:* This is software that allows for a rigorous and analytical approach to optimizing or improving your business processes.
- *Software & hardware for decision management systems:* This is software as a service or pre-configured, out-of-the-box solution that can be integrated into your other systems.

You can build these in a way that makes them all integrated to form your real time interaction management system. A centralized hub and spoke model has been found to be the most effective and the easiest way to deploy new technology on a large scale. When there are too many separate apps and programs, they can confuse the users.

As you know, the people element of RTIM is just as important as the other three pillars, so considerations like this need to be sorted out.

With technology moving so fast, there is a multi-billion dollar market of software makers that can deliver best-in-class options. It makes far more sense to buy an advanced solution that meets your business needs. The benefits include updates, continuous research and development, and ongoing support—and these are big advantages to buying vs. building.

There is no real need to recreate the wheel. If you focus on the type of wheel you need, you can still perform incredibly well. Using the TIPP approach, you will be able to select the ideal software system for your individual business needs.

Implementing Strategy Through RTIM

It has been said that implementing real time interaction management strategically throughout your business is an ideal method of strengthening your customer relationship management systems to produce "total" customer experience management.

The strategic or long-term goals of RTIM are naturally to improve revenue, increase customer retention and satisfaction, and perfect the customer experience. But real time interaction management differs slightly from customer relationship management, and it is important that you know how so that your strategies do not clash.

- *Revenue generation:* Real time interactions are all about getting the sale, which they do by analyzing individual customers and then presenting them with a personalized experience. CRM only supports creating marketing campaigns from this data.

- *Dynamic and static content:* With real time analysis online, your systems will strategically update your website content for specific users. Content is updated while customers use your site. CRM only produces static content for canned experiences.
- *Online and offline data analysis:* Your RTIM system provides you with real time data analysis of your customer's profile using current information. CRM does this offline.
- *Internet and call center:* While real time interaction management software is designed for any type of channel/e-commerce sales, CRM was designed for call centers.
- *Individual and group-centric:* With real time analysis, your systems can achieve one-on-one marketing with individual customer profiles. CRM uses offline analysis and categorizes your customers into groups for marketing campaigns.

I talk about "strategy" like it is something you can choose to ignore, but really everything in real time interaction management is focused on one strategy or another. Implementing these strategies is going to take intimate knowledge of your business, your business systems, and the new cross functional teams that have built and deployed those systems.

Focus on your critical functions to stay on the right track. There are three core critical functions to remember. They are:

1. The ability to store, update, and maintain detailed data for customers.
2. The ability to use real time technology to track customer behavior and movements.
3. The ability to use past, present, and future information to inform decision-making.

From now on, your strategies will involve these three governing factors, and they open up a whole new world of possibilities for your company. If you can target and group which of your customers respond to certain treatments, you will be able to propel your business to new levels of operational efficiency with much higher value customers.

CHAPTER 14
Intelligence: Implementing Interactions

"Our study found that initial implementations are expanding, as are the numbers of tools. However, organizations must establish greater governance and also elevate BI to a strategic level to ensure optimal benefits from their BI investments."

HOWARD DRESNER

How do you go about implementing the business intelligence required to effectively launch and run a quality real time interaction management system? Your business is going to have to face this problem. With the right tools, you are halfway there. The next step must be to ensure that your computer-based techniques are working as they should.

As long as your business intelligence can transform this raw data into useable information, system implementation will run smoother. To ensure that this happens means that shortly after implementation, you will conduct a series of tests and business trials. These will light your way and contribute to establishing your benchmark processes.

Testing Intelligent Interactions

When you begin to test your business intelligence, you move into operational intelligence testing. Operational intelligence involves real time, dynamic business analytics that provide visibility and insight into big datasets. The key here is that operational intelligence must always create continuous insight on an on-going basis.

Testing your new intelligent interactions is going to be something of a process in the beginning, with many changes and alterations in a short space of time. The software that you will be using will constantly provide you with data that will be interpreted by your project management team. Once your data is legible information, or "insights," you can see where the problems lie in the interaction.

Some companies like IBM use rule-based controls or rule engines and A/B testing initially to sort out any immediate problems with their customer interactions. All testing is essentially part of the final optimization process, but it should be seen here as the first step to streamlining your brand new interactions on implementation.

Typically, once the insights have been analyzed and a new interaction process has been pre-tested, simulated, and created, only then does it get rolled out for real world testing. Then the data from this experience is collected along with customer feedback. The interaction is reviewed, revamped, and re-released.

Business Trials

To adequately implement real time interactions, you will need to conduct business trials on your intelligence systems. Once your interactions are operating in the real world, you have the opportunity to gather valuable data that you can use to streamline your intelligence systems on a much more detailed level.

There is no better way to see if your interactions are working than the real marketplace. Be controlled in testing to reduce this business risk. Test vs. control testing is a common approach to many different methodologies like the double blind test or random assignments.

Define trial success criteria up front, and meet periodically to evaluate these trial results. Agree on the metrics for success and the calculation of each metric when working across different organizations. The devil can be in the details, or in this case, the calculations. I have experienced multiple trial efforts fail because they found out mid-trial that the calculations were apples and oranges in terms of comparison.

When your business intelligence is sound, you will make better decisions based on those insights. But how do you know if your current intelligence systems need work? Conduct a business trial that disseminates pieces of data to various people in your project management team. Ask them to draw conclusions or insights from the data, and collect feedback.

It would help if you have one unified system, and your analysts, IT, and business people can simply log on, review the data, and compile reports based on this data. Try representing data in different ways, and ask lists of questions about the data design.

A business trial can really be used to test any aspect of your intelligence systems process. There are five main areas involved with business intelligence that can be properly tested to ensure that the decisions are being made about your customer interactions.

- *Data sourcing:* Extract data from multiple sources of data, whether they are documents, stats, tables, or URL lists. You can run a business trial to test the efficacy of your data sourcing abilities in your business.
- *Data analysis:* Collecting data and analyzing it can be part of a business trial. Review current trends and patterns, and check if your predictive models are working.

- **Situation awareness:** Filter out information that does not matter to make it easier to read by adding this component of business intelligence to a trial or test.
- **Risk assessment:** Understand the risks so that you can take action when you need to. Then decisions can be made correctly at the right times. Summarize your best options in a business trial.
- **Decision support:** Use your information wisely by reviewing your decision management systems and services. Add these to a business trial to see if the decisions being made are the right ones.

Working With Dynamic Testing

Dynamic testing is concerned with assessing the different aspects of an interaction by providing inputs and then assessing the outputs. It is the testing of the dynamic nature of analytics fueling business process. These days—because a business intelligence or data warehousing solution consists of analytics, reporting, data mining, scorecards, dashboards, and predictive analytics—there can be 10 versions of the truth found in this "big data" bundle.

Dynamic testing is also about using real time systems to test across many interactions, applying different treatments to the same interactions to test the efficiency in real time, and then applying that education to interactions in the future. It allows you to test multiple items concurrently.

For example, I read an article in *Wired* magazine[13] about how Obama partnered with Google to make his campaign website amazingly effective to end-users via a series of A/B tests. The result, of course, was an election win, thanks to these new insights, that shocked Obama's team. Their instincts regarding certain

---

13 Brian Christian, The A/B Test: Inside The Technology That's Changing The Rules of Business, http://www.wired.com/business/2012/04/ff_abtesting/

page elements were nearly always off. Just goes to show you how valuable the testing process can be.

In data warehouses, a solution for this was created in the form of dynamic ETL testing, or environmental lab testing. You will need to work with ETL testing at implementation phase to ensure that your interactions are fuelled by the right business intelligence and the performance and timing are acceptable for the business stakeholders.

- The objective of the test is to enable team members to make intelligent decisions based on timely and accurate analysis of big data. The focus needs to be on business transformation applied to data and the validation of that.
- Accuracy and data freshness are key to the success of the entire system. Data needs to be available in real time so that accurate decisions and insights can be drawn from it.
- Data consolidation and retrieval is more important than frequent storage or rare retrieval. Consolidate and model data from multiple sources to support faster retrieval of data over time.
- Because of data security concerns, it is important to maintain the confidentiality of your system information, including customer details and private numbers.
- The history of data needs to be maintained in an often massive space. Data warehouses take up plenty of space as opposed to transactional systems. This historical data needs to be stored and kept secure and safe.

When you work with dynamic testing like this, it can bring a lot of obstacles to light, like performance issues, stale data, scalability issues, and functional problems. Data volume and complexity grow over time, and this needs to be considered.

The testing process can span through the requirement and analysis phase, the design and coding phase, and all the way into the QA and development phases during implementation. This end phase testing is almost always to test data preparation with ETL testing for end-to-end scenarios or with OLAP testing. Report testing is commonly used at this phase as well.

Establishing Benchmark Measurements

Benchmark measurements need to be established during this testing process on implementation of these new customer interactions. The point is to devise a set testing process that can be used to test business intelligence or data warehouse applications.

Establishing benchmark measurements are a very important foundation that your team will have to establish. But here is a testing process that will make it easier for you.

Test Data Preparation

- *Test Data Selection:* Choose a subset of production data to be used. Select based on fixed number, time, or percentage.
- *Generate new test data:* Identify dependencies, constraints, and source tables; understand range of possible values and use data generation tools.

Test Case Design and Execution

- *ETL Testing:* Validate data extraction logic, data transformation logic, and data loading. Data validation, test end-to-end flow, quality validation, accuracy, and completeness.
- *OLAP and Cube Testing:* Check whether the data is mapped and designed correctly in OLAP Cube reports. Validate measures and groups, all the dimensions.
- *Reports Testing:* Verify layout formats, design mock-up, filter attributes, style sheets, and metrics on the report. Verify export functions, drilling, and sorting reports online. You

should also do this for derived metrics and give special attention to reports with non-aggregate-able metrics. Understand each report.

Benchmark measurements can be pulled from any number of these tests by verifying what the most important KPIs, or key performance indicators, are. If it is vital that your data functions in a specific way, you better make sure that this is exactly what it does. If you miss problems at this stage, it could result in poor decisions and ineffective interactions.

Testing these business intelligence apps requires active participation from every member in your project management team. An in-depth knowledge of the entire real time interaction management process is required, so all four pillars of the TIPP approach need to be considered, and all departments (IT, analytics, and functional business teams) should be present.

CHAPTER 15
People: Implementing Interactions

> *"Culture does not change because we desire to change it. Culture changes when the organization is transformed—the culture reflects the realities of people working together every day."*
>
> — FRANCES HESSELBEIN

To effectively implement interactions in your business, you need to make sure that your people are on board during the implementation phase. This is easier said than done. You have an entire company full of people outside your project management team that will not understand why so much has changed in such a short space of time.

It is your job to educate and train these people and introduce them to the new concept of change management. When this amount of transformational "change" occurs, you need to know how to handle it. The good news is that when your employees are on board, the transition will go a lot better for your business.

Change Management 101

What is change management? It is complicated. At any given time, it can refer to software that automates tracking and recording changes to code or IT systems, a process that is meant to help streamline technology-related change, or a tough to teach individual or organizational character that embraces opportunities involved with change.

Essentially, when we talk about change management, it is about managing change in the business context. Your business will be going through an insane amount of change—which as you know, can lead to all sorts of problems, and possibly lack of productivity, among your employees.

To manage change means the same as making changes in a planned, systematic, or managed manner. The goal is always to better implement your new real time interaction management system.

To correctly implement real time interactions, you need to make sure that you have the right focus on how to transition people from working in one type of way to a new kind of role in their job. Your project management team is an example. They must be able to listen, reflect, clarify, lead, and develop your other employees into a workforce that will accept and thrive with real time interaction management systems.

Communications and Training

According to the Change Management Best Practices Benchmarking[14] report, communications planning and training are paramount to any new system rollout. Your project management team will need to take point on this and develop a communication plan that will introduce everyone to the real time interaction management systems.

---

14 Prosci, Change Management Communications Planning, http://www.change-management.com/tutorial-communications.htm

The report found that 40% of all businesses surveyed only had weekly communications—and as you know, a system like RTIM requires a much higher frequency than that. Decide on your communication frequency before moving forward; it should be several times a week.

There are endless ways that teams can communicate with each other. A few are focus groups, bulletin boards, demonstrations, newsletters, communication trees, presentations, one-on-one meetings, FAQs, department meetings, posters, emails, workshops—the list goes on and on.

The report found that one-on-one communication was the most effective—including discussions, demonstrations, presentations, and group or team meetings. After this, email seems to be the next best method of company-wide communication.

To implement these new interactions into your business model means that your project team will also need to decide WHO should deliver the message. In order of importance, first the CEO, then the employee's supervisor, the executive manager, senior manager, department head, and change management leaders should be the dominant communicators.

In this instance, the CEO would be an effective choice initially, followed by the sponsor and project management team. The next thing to decide would be the KIND of message you are going to relay to your employees company-wide.

Important messages to communicate could be anything from the current status and reasons behind the changes, the new company vision after the change, the basics of what is changing, how and when it will change, the expectation of change, and incremental updates on the implementation of change.

Communication with the people in your company is very important to the success of your real time interaction management system implementation. You should also focus on individuals within your company to let them know how all of this change will affect what they do. It is a monumental task, but on implementation, it must be performed.

Process and Interaction Compliance

Part of preparing for change management when you implement these real time interaction management systems involves ensuring that your employees comply with your new business rules and processes. This can be outstandingly tricky, as it is nearly impossible to have eyes on everyone at any given time.

What you can do is present an incentive-based system for the leadership of your company to ensure that they have eyes where you need them. The moment your new system is launched, you will want your branch managers making sure that employees are taking advantage of the real time interactions in the real world.

As with any new system, there needs to be some sort of control model for the risk and compliance side of performance management. A healthy respect for these business rules is essential, but understanding them is one thing. Compliance is a whole different matter.

You need to "walk a tightrope" with compliance, balancing understanding with performance to get the best from your employees. The good news is that along with interaction analytics comes a method of tracking and monitoring the behavior of your employees, wherever they are using your systems.

This data can then be processed into business intelligence, and you will be able to see exactly who has been using the new system and who is still struggling to use it. Setting KPIs in this regard will go a long way in ironing out future concerns as you launch updates and add-ons in the coming years.

Compliance is one of the most dominant metrics your business can measure at this stage, and it relates directly to the implementation of your interactions. Features like real time monitoring and alerting will only help leaders address these problems for your company on a micro-scale.

If too many faults are found, key staff can run through the training program again—using one of the more intimate training methods (one-on-one) to gain a better understanding of the way the systems work. From there, it should be a simple matter of practice makes perfect.

CHAPTER 16

Process: Implementing Interactions

"When something goes wrong, it's either because there is too much process, too little process or the wrong process. Likewise, when something goes right, it's because the right resources (people or systems) were engaged at the right time."

MIHNEA GALETEANU

You have reached the stage when you will be implementing interactions according to the TIPP approach, beginning with the deployment of new processes. Whether you are using a Six Sigma system or a general Agile deployment method, the goal is the same—to roll out processes that result in immediate and long-term improvement.

These improvements can and should affect the four pillars of the TIPP approach. A single business process can make your employees lives easier, harness previously unused business intelligence, and add a piece of technology to your systems. Here is how you will go about ensuring success as you implement these new interactions.

Deploying New Processes

Do you remember the process maps we discussed earlier? In the Six Sigma approach, a deployment flowchart is often used as a business process mapping tool that outlines the steps your people will take to roll out a sponsor-approved process.

Business architecture activities need to be executed, like forming new groups and organizing resources to execute new processes. Your architecture will need to be developed according to your needs. You will have to describe the service strategy or interaction and the organizational, functional, process, information, and geographical aspects of the business environment based on pre-formulated principles, strategic drivers, and established business goals.

Knowledge of the business architecture is vital for architecture work in any area, including data and technology. It needs to already be catered for in the other organizational process plans. Create a detailed plan that will help you execute and optimize the activities that have to take place in this section. An activity model is also called a business process model, and this is the document you will need to prepare. Included in this document may be any of the following activities:

- Face to face interviews
- Process map analysis
- Key performance indicators
- Department interactions
- Process prioritization

These are called cross functional flowcharts as they are intended to be used by everyone in the project management team, including IT, business, and analytics departments. These flowcharts highlight the relationships between the people involved in deploying the new process as well as the process flow itself.

It is common during this process to showcase areas of duplication, unnecessary processing, and obvious inefficiency. These great flowcharts are used as interfaces between the project management teams so that delays and miscommunications are avoided or reduced.

Microsoft Visio is often a software tool used in this instance to create these flowcharts, though they can be brainstormed in a meeting and developed by hand. In order for these flowcharts to be of any use, however, they must be detailed.

On the other hand, if you choose to use an Agile deployment method, you will focus on an implementation process that prioritizes interactions between the project team and the process users. There is a lot of hands-on implementation with software at this point as well. Agile process deployment is fast and configurable and saves you time.

With a simple to use interface, stakeholders are involved at every level of the project—from planning and scoping the process, to configuring it, to exercising and reviewing it, to refining it in terms of customer usage—and then deploying it on a company-wide scale. Immediate access to functionality at the end of this process results in additional value.

A well-designed deployment system results in minimized risk, tangible benefits, decreased total cost of ownership, and simple system integration and data migration. With the right leadership support and resource allocation, within months, you can introduce a proven new business process to every branch of your company. Once the foundation is laid, that timeframe goes to days and weeks to adjust a complete process across the company—a very real new business capability.

Measuring Processes

How is it possible to measure the cumulative intelligence of a new business process? Jim Sinur[15] theorized that it can be done

---

15 Jim Sinur, Measuring the Cumulative Intelligence of a Process, http://jimsinur.blogspot.ca/2013/05/measuring-cumulative-intelligence-of.html?m=1

based on five continuum lines. Intelligent processes are created by monitoring and measuring different factors that create a shape that represents the intelligence of a process.

It is called the cumulative process intelligence quotient. There are five points to this model, including raw intelligence, social intelligence, autonomy, visualization, and agility. The first of the five—raw intelligence—contains another five levels that create a framework for measurement. The others contain smaller levels as well.

- *Raw intelligence:* Handling expected business logic, recognizing emerging events and patterns, analyzing alternatives with poly analytics, machine assistance, or learning and finally digital direction—these levels can be used to measure the importance or IMPACT of a raw process that you have implemented.
- *Social intelligence:* Basic collaboration, skills-driven collaboration, crowd-sourcing, social network analysis, and ranked better practices are all levels of social intelligence that can be used to measure the IMPACT of a social process.
- *Autonomy:* Programmed behavior, permitted actions, act first—then notify, act with constraints and goals, and interactive independent action are all levels of autonomous intelligence that can be used to measure the IMPACT of individual processes.
- *Visualization:* Push visualization, custom subscribed visualization, warning and notification, simulated driven visualization, and gamification (training simulator) are all levels of visual intelligence that can be used to measure the IMPACT of visual processes.
- *Agility:* Explicit parameters, explicit policies and rules, dynamic sequencing of services, dynamic milestones, and goal direction are all levels of agile intelligence that can be

used to measure the IMPACT of agile processes. This focuses on real time intelligence as well.

These measures are still being developed, though there is a distinct need for quantifiable measures to determine how smart our processes are. In the meantime, use this framework to identify patterns and trends and generate data that will help you determine whether or not a specific process has become successful in an ever-changing market.

The cumulative process intelligence quotient has been used on traditional applications to determine that they do not have the kind of process intelligence required to meet the changing business needs in future markets. Applications and augmented technology like rule engines are far better suited to handle such an adaptive, evolving market.

Every new process that you roll out needs to be run through the cumulative process intelligence quotient to determine its value to your company in the short and long term.

Establishing Benchmark Measurements

A benchmark measurement is an age-old method of ensuring that all processes that you implement are striving to be the best in their class. Benchmarking actually represents an evolving component of management practice in total quality management operations. It can be used in this context to guarantee that the measurements you are performing are always contributing the most to the eventual end goal of the business—profit.

The way you establish your benchmark measurements will depend on your goals, management structure, organizational structure, industry, business culture, and philosophy.

The Planning Phase of Benchmarking:

- Take some time and identify which measurements need to be benchmarked.

- Compare these benchmarks with the benchmarks from other companies.
- Determine what the best data collection method may be for this.

The Analysis Phase of Benchmarking:

- Determine what your current performance gap may be.
- Based on your data, predict future performance levels of each measurement.

The Integration Phase of Benchmarking:

- Communicate your findings, and gain acceptance from the project team.
- Establish your functional business goals.

The Action Phase of Benchmarking:

- Develop your measurement plan of action.
- Implement your plans and monitor your progress.
- Test and recalibrate your measurements.

The Mature Phase of Benchmarking:

- Integrate your new practices into your process.

You will be able to create a process map for benchmarking that can act as your working plan for continually improving your benchmark measurement processes. If this breaks down, the entire system stops working. That is why it is essential to recycle this process over and over again.

To adequately establish benchmark measurements for determining the value of new processes, this cycle must not end. To be a customer-centric business is to be a business that guarantees every new process is tested and functioning for the benefit of your customer base. This is how you retain customers, improve relationships, and continue to grow.

You may want to begin with a readiness test to determine whether your organization is capable of starting and sustaining these benchmark measurement processes. If it is not, you have your first step towards eventually creating a benchmark process map.

CHAPTER 17
Transitioning to Business as Usual

> *"Real-time decision-making also has to be vetted with domain knowledge, human experience and common sense, to validate the viability of analytics results. Decisions make a positive difference for the enterprise only if they are based on accurate intelligence."*
>
> **JULIE HUNT**

The TIPP approach consists of technology, intelligence, people, and process. Once you have taken the time to learn all you can about this approach and have implemented it into your business, it will be your responsibility to ensure that you maintain your improved performance levels.

This radical and revolutionary approach to moving from an enterprise-centric business to a customer-centric business has two defining features: continuous improvement and consistent execution. If you follow the approach, you will transform the definition of "business as usual."

Making TIPP a Part of Daily Business

With these new systems in place, you will be focused on improving everything, from the technology infrastructure that you use, the business intelligence that you create, the people you hire and train—and the processes that you adapt, map out, and execute. Everything is directed at a better customer experience and a close customer relationship between you and your existing consumer base. In other words, you will be focused on consistent execution.

Daily business at this point is cutthroat. New data will surface all the time that needs to be tested. Your business rules will be challenged. Your business process management ability will be tested in the field. There will be a never ending river of data that has to be interpreted and integrated into your ongoing real time interaction management system.

Intelligent interactions are not about starting with the absolute best. They are about understanding that the four pillars that keep real time interactions going are outlined in this TIPP approach. Wherever you begin, the destination is the same—success. This is how real time interaction management systems need to be designed.

Over time, you will learn incredible things about your individual customers. You will realize that customer-centric decisioning and predictive analytics will shift your focus down to the very last person or process in your company. With a proactive business intelligence system on your side, you will be able to evolve with your market.

The only way to continue along these lines is to constantly remind your people that it is up to them to keep the TIPP approach in mind when they plan, design, implement, update, alter, or launch something new. It is far easier to maintain the success of one singular, unified system than to attempt to do the same with segmented, uncommunicative departments.

There will be subtle differences in the way you conduct business, but they will be meaningful, and you will see the impact of these decisions and changes immediately as well as over time. The real challenge will happen at this stage. Anyone can implement this new technology, intelligence, process methodology and people-centric plan into their business.

Sustaining and developing the model is something entirely different. At this stage, you see how each division comes together to achieve the goals of the company.

PART V

360 Degree Vision: Sustaining RTIM as a Business Capability

CHAPTER 18

Strategy and Technology: Engagement and Commitment to RTIM

"BPM isn't just about automation—it's about transforming and improving the way that your organization operates. BPM is about changing the way you engage your knowledge workers to drive positive, meaningful change across the enterprise."

ANONYMOUS

Some of the best business capabilities are the most difficult to sustain over time. Real time interaction management can be this way if your employees are not always 100% dedicated and committed to the new system.

Your technology is managed and governed by the people in your business, as is your strategy. To continue to improve your real time interaction management system means that you will have to guarantee that none of these pillars fail to support the business.

Successful Technology and Strategy: Consumed by Process

If you are going to be successful at keeping your technology and strategy aligned with your business needs, then you need to understand that business process management is what has to be carefully monitored.

Business process and rules are really two sides of the same coin. One describes what will happen next, and the other lays out the constraints for what happens next. Though machines are not all-knowing, they definitely allow people to get on with their work by taking care of processes that can be automated and automatically updated.

This is why we say that successful technology is consumed by strategic process. Business processes that are associated with technology are running in the background, keeping the business moving forward automatically.

Machines, however, will always need to be monitored, adjusted, improved, and changed according to the needs of the customer and the business. It is your responsibility to always have the best possible technology and executable strategies in place to lighten the load for your people.

When your technology is current, flexible, agile, and adaptable, it goes a long way in making sure that real time interactions are done exactly as your stakeholder team imagined they would. And these are systems after all; errors, issues, and clashes will arise that your teams will have to fix. Stay on top of these systems, and they will sustain your real time interaction management goals.

Successful Process Is Consumed by Aligned People

For proper engagement and commitment to real time interaction management, technology only makes up one side of the story. The other side is the people that are supposed to be aligned with your business processes.

That is why we say that successful process is consumed by aligned people. Without the human element working towards the successful implementation of your real time interactions, you can never hope to sustain a complex data system like this.

When people become sloppy, technology falls out of date. Extras that could have sped up the system are overlooked. Updates are not integrated. Knowledge is not effectively transitioned as people move in and out of different roles and responsibilities across the team.

A real time interaction management system can be a difficult thing to keep going over time. That is why you will also need your business process professionals and interaction execution channels to do their job—which will be to ensure that everyone else is staying on top of their game.

- *Using business process management software:* When the hard parts are in action—thanks to quality BPM software—people do not have to do the heavy lifting. Business cycles are moving at an alarming rate, and technology, strategy, and the processes themselves are constantly evolving. Make your technology platform do the hard work.

- *Revolutionize how your business delivers value to customers:* Quick fixes and fake improvements to your processes will not do anything for your long-term goals. Competition is high, and to keep it under control, you have to maximize every process. You need an outside view of the customer and how work is performed for this to happen.

- *Use business metaphors to engage the business:* You have to educate and engage with the people in your business to get them involved in the transformation process. Ensuring active participation and leadership from your executives is going to be hard to pull off. Taking that and translating it into broader business engagement is challenge enough.

When your people are aligned to your business goals, they can be your greatest long-term asset. But never forget these steps in the chain. When it comes to human channels, of all the four pillars, technology and strategy and people are the most important. They are the drivers behind effective business process management—the machines because they lighten the load and the people because they conduct the interactions.

CHAPTER 19
Intelligence: Engagement and Commitment to RTIM

> *"You can't really determine the value of BI or data warehousing unless they're linked to a particular initiative to improve decision-making. Otherwise, you'll have no idea how the information and tools are being used."*
>
> — TOM DAVENPORT

As I mentioned previously, processes are the how, and business rules are the framework in which the how is executed. All businesses need to focus on the rules they will create around their real time interaction management systems.

If you are going to be engaged and committed to your real time interactions, your business intelligence needs to feed your business rules management system. This is the system that will help your people correctly program your technology and conduct the daily processes they need to carry out for system success.

Interaction Business Rules Management

Your business process management software will be some flavor of "rules-based" and will contain a business rules management system that will work alongside your BPM software to keep your interactions happening in real time.

For a smart process management solution, you need great business rules and analytic models. These are the "brains" of your business process management system. These rules can be applied to an organization, individuals, and online- or systems-based interactions. Just like the brain, they are constantly "learning" and evaluating. The business will need to own and manage the intelligence of the interaction, and by doing so, they will inherently be managing the rules and logic of the system.

Business rules are better understood by the people in your business who are accountable for them, which means more fluent cooperation, fewer errors, and a significant reduction in implementing real time interactions. These rules systems have execution flow, cross-referencing tools, interactive testing, and great reporting features as well.

A business rules platform, for example, separates business logic from your business apps and gives you centralized control over that logic. This can increase the flexibility of your business processes and improve coordination across all of your current systems.

Dynamic business rules will automate your workflow management, and they offer a wide range of decisioning rule types like decision maps, tables, and trees. There is forward and backward chaining, data transformation rules that allow data to pass from dissimilar IT systems, and declarative rules that compute value based on changes in other values.

Altogether your business rules management system gives your business users and analysts the ability to update and change the rules that drive decision services. This does not interrupt the IT department, and they are left free to focus on more important things like major development efforts (foundational updates, the extension of the platform into new business channels and functions, that kind of thing).

Your business must be able to transparently see the decisions, and ultimately the interactions that take place, by way of the systems you have implemented. This output will give you insight into the rules' effectiveness. Without this transparency, the business will be looking at a "black box," and it will risk the long-term successes that are supposed to follow.

This is a challenging area and will require consistent process and people alignment to effectively execute this "back office" type of effort. I usually give my rule activity reports to my cross functional governance teams as well as the specific business owners accountable for the activity. From there, you can set up new trial efforts to test and implement new rule changes and adaptations.

The New Type of Business: Resource – Business / Tech/ Analytics

There is a new type of business resource that you will need for the new business world you just created, and it belongs almost exclusively to the platform management team that contains members or experts from your business, technology, and analytics departments.

The new resources you hire to build this team will likely be people that have career depth in both business operations (process orientated) and technology, ideally with an analytics background. Where would you find these people? Some you can get from the general marketplace, consulting at a premium—or they may be your new CEO. If you are lucky, you could find a person or two who can cover these areas, but chances are you will have to invest significantly in talent.

Developing people is usually a cost of doing business today. Their resources will need to be on the cutting edge of learning and applying this capability. In an ideal world, your implemented RTIM capability means that your business now has all of the levers and dials to control and optimize your business.

You will need the right people to execute the business changes; people who know what they are doing and understand the ramifications if they are not executed flawlessly. These people should speak at all levels across the organization and across business functions.

These platform owners and supporting resources are like garden keepers. Remember the garden analogy? They maintain the soil by providing the water and nutrients needed to grow the garden to maturity. The business functions are like individual gardeners coming to grow the things their specific businesses need.

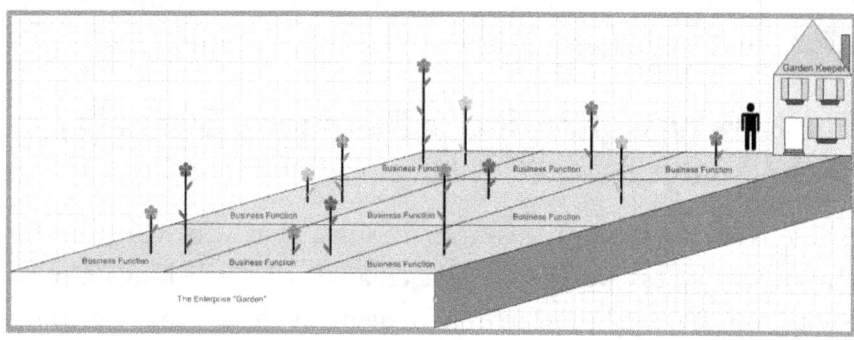

A good platform owner's resources are always evaluating other gardens in the community to see what is and what is not working and finding the best resources to "splice" and clone better results. When they find things that work, they share it with other business gardeners to supplement their business when it aligns with their garden.

They help them to see the opportunity for their garden (business), but then they work together to architect the new area of garden that will assist in business growth. RTIM is like a garden; your business will need an entity to own and maintain the garden. Business gardeners will need to be aware of how and what to plant in the garden.

A business resource is first and foremost supposed to provide the organization with the means to perform its business processes. Real time interactions are the processes we are talking about here. In order for them to work efficiently, you have to develop your team as a new kind of business resource.

These close-knit, expert teams from different departments have the depth of knowledge, experience, and reach to effect positive change on your real time interaction management systems at any given time.

They will be the first people to know if there is a problem in any one of the multiple departments that will run your real time interaction systems. A cross functional team has many benefits, but lately businesses are looking at these teams as a part of their overall business intelligence.

After all, it matters WHO interprets the data and what sort of insights they produce. If a cross functional team like this can sit together and discuss the meaning of a particular piece of information or business intelligence, surely they will be able to come up with more applicable insights that a single person could not.

In this way, they expand and improve the intelligence of the business, lending a more three dimensional perspective to the big data problem. There are many reasons to shape your cross functional team into a business resource:

- *Diversity:* Take advantage of different backgrounds, education levels, experience, skills sets, and talent in a diverse group that consists of these core people.
- *Accuracy:* When the team looks at data or at a conflict, there is a much higher accuracy rate as intelligence is pooled together before a decision is made.
- *Shared purpose:* Having a shared purpose promotes collaboration on more than just your real time systems. Teams will naturally begin to communicate more as they transition into roles that do not have any limitations.

The new type of business resource is clearly human intelligence with enterprise business expertise; in particular, intelligence from people that know something specific about what they do. The IT department, analytics department, and business department teams are perfectly positioned to join forces and become a potent new force for business profitability in your company.

Balancing the Skill Sets

Now that you understand that human intelligence is going to be a large part of business intelligence for your company, it is crucial that you learn how to balance the skill sets of the many different people in your cross functional teams.

Your teams will be helping your business determine the HOW of every single process that needs to be carried out in order for real time interactions to take place. If you consider that their main goals are to improve the quality of decision making, increase organizational flexibility and productivity, and generate more business revenue, then you can see why it is important to balance the scales when you put teams together.

Your goal for achieving balance is to put together a team that is creative and highly innovative while still able to carry out the functions that your real time interaction management systems demand of them.

- *Balance technical and functional expertise:* Take a closer look at their educational backgrounds, knowledge strengths, training, unique perspectives, and experience over the span of their careers.
- *Balance problem solving and decision making skills*: Investigate who in your departments has the ability to best identify problems, evaluate options, act on opportunities, and move forward with them.
- *Balance interpersonal skills or compatibility:* Delve into your potential team member's communication abilities,

temperament, IQ, personalities, style, support, and intervention skills and how they facilitate others.

Do not be afraid to mix it up. For example, if you have no one in your IT department that can plan effectively, begin training in this regard for the most likely candidates immediately. In the future, make sure that those in leadership positions in IT can in fact plan effectively.

You will be required to form large and small teams for various tasks related to business intelligence and real time interaction management systems. Shake things up, and surprise yourself. The better balanced your teams are, the better they will work together for the good of your real time interactions and eventual business goals.

In an ideal situation, your prospective team members should volunteer for the job and then be interviewed based on a predefined set of criteria. Then you can assemble your cross functional team and see how it works.

Cross-Functional Visibility and Neutrality

There are two features that cross functional teams bring to your business intelligence when they start working together as a unit. These are increased levels of visibility and neutrality. Both are required constantly in business intelligence to properly engage with your customers, fix system errors, and make the necessary changes in real time.

A cross functional team gives you greater visibility in your company, specifically with the intelligence that your company generates and acts on. Business intelligence is a very machine-based discipline, but as we have established, every piece of data needs to be adequately interpreted.

When you can see exactly HOW a piece of data has been interpreted, you will understand why it has been working as a real time interaction or not working at all. Whenever something goes wrong with real time interactions, it is important that you are able to retrace your steps back to the data and thought process that resulted in certain decisions being made.

When you have this kind of visibility in your software systems and decision management systems, change is a lot easier to implement. When these insights are universally visible throughout the business, it saves you time and money and helps your other cross functional teams make the decisions they need to make in order to move forward.

Neutrality is an underestimated but highly desirable side effect that cross functional teams bring to your business intelligence. If an individual, say an IT employee, was tasked with reviewing certain data and compiling insight reports, a few things would go wrong.

First of all, they would keep their department's best interests in mind and would not have a rounded business or analytics view of the company. In fact, they may completely disregard the needs of these two other essential departments because they do not know any better.

If you do not have neutrality, you run the risk of one department or function turning your cross functional business capability into a very expensive "sales" tool if, say, the sales, marketing, or collections team was left to build as they pleased. The REAL benefits do not come until you can effectively cross function in a way conducive to a human interaction.

The result is a very one-sided view of the data. The insights that are drawn from it are biased, and this is not going to help anyone create effective real time interactions. What you want is a few expert team members from each department working on the same data. They will be forced to give a neutral perspective based on the overall business view.

CHAPTER 20

People: Engagement and Commitment to RTIM

"After each customer interaction, notice if you gave them a 'happy to see you' kind of experience."

MARILYN SUTTLE

Decision management is supposed to move your business from your basic business intelligence model to a predictive analytics model that is centered more around operational intelligence. Big data is not going away, so your people need be fully engaged and committed to real time interaction management systems.

You know that it is important that your decisions are agile, adaptive, and analytics-based. But now you have to examine who owns your interactions, what sort of incentives can drive positive change, and how cross functional governance will work in your favor.

Interaction Ownership

Who owns your interactions? Some experts claim that your sales team owns what your customers get to experience. While this is true to a certain degree, the fact remains that like your new intelligence teams, ownership is becoming cross functional. An interaction is therefore "owned" by the company as a whole and every individual that works there.

But of course, this makes measurement and control nearly impossible. So instead, you will assign ownership to your senior executive sponsor, your CEO, and your key project management team. This is because your CEO is the owner of the business, your sponsor is supposed to oversee your RTIM team, and your team creates, implements, adjusts, deploys, and maintains your real time interactions.

There are four kinds of customer interaction that are based on your process standardization and level of customer engagement. These are "business as usual," "threats to cost efficiency," "predictable customer lifecycle events," and "surprise, trials, and tribulations."

1. *Business as usual:* This involves lots of repetitiveness and opportunity for standardization of process. This is a routine customer transaction that has very predictable outcomes.
2. *Predictable customer lifecycle events:* It is easy to standardize these interactions, but they are not routine, such as when a customer receives his first bill from you for example.
3. *Threats to cost efficiency:* These interactions cannot be standardized, and they consist of things that were not planned—like an unusual event. An example may be when a customer's identity is stolen and someone uses it to book into a hotel. That hotel group would have to manually deal with the problem.
4. *Surprises, trials, and tribulations:* This kind of interaction is a real threat to your business's bottom line. When a customer

is highly engaged with your brand but there are no processes for performing the task required, this means that your process mapping has not been done effectively.

Incentive Alignment

Incentives have long been the motivating factor for people across all departments in business. To properly manage a company's human capital, it is important that you take incentive alignment into account.

Right now there is a clear separation in decision-making and ownership in businesses across the globe. Usually, key leadership members are given incentives to improve the board of director's bottom line. But these interests are not always for the good of the customer and therefore need to be realigned.

When a company does well, their CEO usually receives a massive financial bonus as it is part of their contract. This is why the leadership in a company is always so concerned with money instead of exploring alternative and potentially better methods of bringing in revenue that are non-traditional.

What you want is a team-based incentive system that motivates everyone in your project management team to continuously push for better customer interactions. The link between financial incentive and the customer experience must be made.

This is because it is the most direct route to inflating your revenue without forcing your teams to compromise what they are doing just for the sake of lining the business owner's pockets. There are seven categories of incentive systems that you can align to your new business purpose–customer experience.

These categories can be anything from team profit sharing, team goal-based incentive systems, team skill incentive systems, and team discretionary bonus systems to team member skill incentive systems, team member merit incentive systems, and team member goal incentive systems.

Aligning these incentive systems to the ultimate goals of your company will pay off in the long run. They will motivate your leadership to keep working towards the best customer experience possible fuelled by quality interactions that are built into your processes. If you do not align these, be ready for the "flavor of the day" experience with your RTIM system.

Incentive alignment is just another way of mentioning that you need to accelerate the performance of your human assets. Throughout history, incentives have been the most effective method of doing this. Use it to your advantage by implementing team-based incentives that will improve your real time interaction management systems.

Cross-Functions and Channels

Multi-channel interactions are happening every day as the retail environment expands and moves into the online space. If your people are going to improve productivity and profitability, then you need a more collaborative approach with these channels.

A cross functional solution is what is required due to the increasing complexity of your competition and distribution channels. Customer dissatisfaction is almost a direct result of not having cross functional teams that are working towards the ultimate customer experience on all levels.

In marketing alone, you have the need for many experts in your business so that a quality marketing campaign can be launched and deemed successful. There is merchandising, finance, planning, distribution or channel strategy, brand marketing, and creative work that need to be completed.

Instead of passing the project around to the various silos in your business, would it not make more sense to use these cross functional teams (or the creation of specific teams) to get it right the first time? You cannot afford to have a one-sided perspective in business anymore.

The various distribution channels alone call for a more cross functional approach to executing real time interactions. There is email, call center, face-to-face, website, social media, and advertising that can all count as interactions. Anything that the customer experiences from your brand constitutes an interaction.

That is why it is important that you put together cross functional business teams as a general rule once your real time interaction management systems have been integrated into your business. If you are going to be fully committed to making these interactions propel your revenue upward, this is what you need to do.

If you are lazy about it, your real time interaction management system could turn into a nightmare. Wrong data and incorrect decision-making will result in poor customer experiences, and you will rapidly LOSE customers instead of harvesting existing customers to their maximum potential.

Cross-Functional Governance

Cross functional governance is the future of your business and the business of your direct competition. Governance simply means "a system of government," but an easier way of defining it may be "the organization of management."

In other words, governance means the goals, principles, and organization charts that determine who can make the big decisions along with the rules and policies that define or constrain what these leaders are able to do.

Cross functional governance is basically an effective, proactive form of management that enforces continuous improvement in your business processes while delivering value to your customers. It is what I have been saying all along—instead of a single "leader" making the rules and working towards the business goals, teams need to do it.

When you have cross functional teams of leaders working towards a better customer experience, everyone wins in the end.

There are five key elements of cross functional governance that you can implement as you see fit:

1. *Measurement:* Have your entire cross functional team measure your process performance on a continuous basis.
2. *Ownership:* Your business should appoint a process "owner" for every cross functional process you are impacting with RTIM in your business. You can find these candidates as you establish your cross functional teams.
3. *Control:* A process owner needs to be a collaborative leader, involving their cross functional teams and making group decisions for the benefit of the business.
4. *Accountability:* Your process owners have to be leaders as accountability is essential in any governance structure. Cross functional process performance needs to matter to the person or people that own the process.
5. *Support:* All process owners will need support, training, and team collaboration to keep them going. You can also form process councils to guarantee the integrity of an important customer interaction.

This is cross functional governance in a nutshell. There are still hierarchies, but they encourage the use of preformed teams to assist in the continuous improvement process. When one individual owns a process, they will care about it more and can be held accountable to the performance. This is the "one throat to choke" so to speak. They will also use their cross functional teams to keep that process working at its best.

CHAPTER 21
Process: Engagement and Commitment to RTIM

> *"Learning is the beginning of wealth. Learning is the beginning of health. Learning is the beginning of spirituality. Searching and learning is where the miracle process all begins."*
>
> — JIM ROHN

After the measurement phase of a Six Sigma approach, there is the analyze phase. This phase is mainly concerned with establishing baseline and future state performance standards while beginning investigation into the best sub-process variation sources.

When you have reached this level, it is your job to commit to the business processes in real time interaction management and engage with the steps that are taken in order to produce more successful outcomes now and in the future for your organization.

Measurements and Observations

Once the measurements have been taken for a specific process using a Six Sigma-like approach, you need to analyze or observe the data that has been collected. The available data will be prepared and input into another software tool. This tool will provide you with capability scores so that you can evaluate process capabilities.

Now that you have a cross functional governance team, it will be key to give them facts to work with. Important processes and metrics will need to be measured and observed frequently. Observations, both good and bad, will need to be shared often on an ongoing basis with the governing teams and process owners. Decisions will be made, and the TIPP approach will be used to construct changes to the customer interactions.

From here, standard deviation and the mean of the data are calculated to produce the data sample. As the Six Sigma approach relies heavily on analyzing data distributions relative to normal distributions around the mean, a Six Sigma score is derived from these calculations resulting from various known factors.

The goal is to eventually enter into a continuous improvement loop with business process management and a Six Sigma approach. Hypothesis testing and analysis can be done on exported data. Any changes to business rules or processes can be propagated to the live production process. Once run through the statistical tool, the process capability can be analyzed.

The next step of the DMAIC process is concerned with setting future state performance standards. Benchmarking is completed. Performance objectives are established so that key performance indicators are not violated. Then comes the identification of variation sources. These are based on historical data, which factors to further investigate during the improvement phase, and which tools to use.

Process maps, hypothesis testing, regression analysis, fishbone diagrams, and a Pareto chart are all used at this stage to determine which sources are good to use. You will be able to organize processes, decision rules, expressions, and service levels using a multi-dimensional hierarchy.

The why, when, where, what, who, and user roles are identified so that the organization of businesses rules run along a number of dimensions. The appropriate control rule is applied based on a particular situation. This is how you adequately measure and observe Six Sigma business processes using a Process Analyzer.

On-going Testing and Learning Environment

Though the first two phases are concerned with finding business problems, this phase is involved with improvements. Experimentation and investigation make way for solutions to be found and applied on a continuous basis.

These supportive tools and process systems lend themselves to an on-going testing and learning environment. The key potential sources of failure are screened and narrowed down. Then the true nature of the relationship between the vital source and the outcome is plotted.

In this phase, you will determine the dependence of process performance on input parameters, and you will determine the limits required for process inputs to keep the output in a specific range. There are many capabilities that support this, including property definition, agent technology that monitors and processes, testing and piloting, and support for process versioning.

Once this is done, care is taken to eliminate as many "issues" as possible before conducting experiments. Past data, common sense, and experience are used to consolidate the candidates into the final few "main concerns." Then you will screen for potential causes using Six Sigma-like technology to do so.

Now it is time to determine what the optimal settings of the input parameter should be. This step is about discovering the variable relationships by using a set of testing functions.

Everything until now has been to determine the x and y values, which will serve as set points for the parameters of your future process designs.

With experiments, pilots, and simulations, you will establish operating tolerances. Then you will discover relationships between variables and these operating tolerances. Once established, users can create pilot procedures and policies and test, measure, experiment, and apply them to business logic. At this point, decision rules, expressions, constraints, service levels, and other features will make up the automated application.

Dozens of improvement processes can be executed using the process evaluation software. Software is flexible and will quickly modify processes and set rules on these processes that make sense and do not negatively affect work flow.

These small improvements are quickly implemented over time by the project managers using the Six Sigma approach. These improvements are constant and continuous, and they generate a sense of control within the project team.

An on-going testing and learning environment is instrumental in ensuring that your existing business processes are always validated and valuable and that any new processes will fit into your current business practice and context without causing problems or interrupting the natural flow of your daily business.

Demonstrating ROI

It is common practice to be able to demonstrate the benefits and results of your information systems, or IT, investments that your company owns. This ROI represents the key measure of business decisions and investment priorities. You need to be able to justify the business case for business process management, especially with the software that you use.

In the previous examples, I used a Six Sigma approach to testing and determining which new business processes would benefit your company. If you are going to justify using this approach, you will need to know how to estimate ROI on business process management.

Keep in mind that ROI is best expressed in terms of monetary benefit. Successful business process management projects always result in increased finances because of process automation and consistent improvements.

- *Identify your problems and opportunities:* With a Six Sigma approach, the data is there for you to use whenever you need it. The value of your projects should be high and the complexity level reasonably low.
- *What is the scope of the project to be improved?* Define the scope of the process and the frameworks that will be used to measure inputs and outputs.
- *Estimate the soft and hard benefits:* Hard benefits include cost, productivity, and time, and they always affect new process measurement. Soft benefits include visibility, transparency, improved reporting, and risk mitigation.
- *What is the extent of your investment?* You will need an accurate estimate of the investment required in people, training, software, and hardware. The cost of doing business needs to be calculated with each new business process.
- *Reframing the cost benefits:* Once your sponsor understands why the investment is needed and what the benefits of deployment are, you need to mock up a chart that presents this information in an easy-to-read way. Complete a worksheet detailing time, quality, and productivity and how it will reduce costs, increase customer satisfaction, and improve compliance and risk management.
- *Gaining commitment through presentation:* To adequately demonstrate your ROI, create a summary statement of each estimated benefit in terms of revenue increase and overall

cost reduction. This will boldly present the breakeven point for the investment vs. ROI calculation. When accurately planned, scoped, and deployed, the value of business process management quickly exceeds the investment needed—which looks great on a chart and also builds confidence and alignment with your stakeholders as to where the goal is.

The process of estimating and being able to demonstrate the return on investment for new business process management projects is key to getting the most out of technology in this digital age. Your competitive advantage is at stake here. The longer you do not have a functional business process management system with a way to test and improve your business processes, the weaker your business becomes—your competition is banking on this.

Key Performance Indicators

Finding out which KPIs to define when entering the business process management cycle is essential to supporting the business case for deciding whether or not the new initiative is viable or a waste of time.

KPIs are vital tools used to measure and control the performance of any given process. Without them, you will never be able to determine what the ROI of a specific process may be. The only good KPI is a strategic one. In order for a KPI to define your business process management system, it needs to be linked to your corporate strategy.

If your company has developed a strategy to improve your operational functionality, you need a way to quantify this. But how do you turn this goal into a KPI? You first have to define your strategy and break it down. Let's say you want to boost operational performance in your call center. Two goals from this plan may be to reduce costs and improve customer service.

These smaller goals are pretty solid, and they are closer to being KPIs than your main strategy. But to monitor performance, you need metrics—numbers. Goals can become metrics, however, like in the case of the call center costs. A good KPI for this would be a timeline that shows cost percentages for a set amount of time.

Once this KPI is outlined, you can break it down into calculations, dimensions, and systems of origin. You will identify the system that provides the data for the KPI calculation—your cost accounting system. The dimensions will be business units, functions, and time periods—all ways to sort the information.

Finally, the calculation would take costs incurred in previous years into account and the costs incurred with the new process in place. The most important thing here is the direct link between strategy and numbers. A small KPI like cost reduction in the call center affects the goal to reduce overall costs and the main goal of improving operational functionality.

Your KPIs need to be performance driven and monitored. Even though you will always need numbers, do not let it become a numbers game. If you focus too much on meeting those set numbers, you will lose sight of other opportunities as they arise.

This method of integrating your KPIs into your overall corporate strategy is very important for ensuring that you stay on track and aligned with your overall goals. If you can trace a direct path from a small KPI to your main goal or strategy, then you can almost guarantee that any improvements will affect your main goal.

You will also have the added benefit of "aligned KPIs," which can be accurately measured to determine how well your business is doing overall. When your KPIs are not aligned, they are not useful for gauging the performance of an organization. A lot of this information that you thought was crucial can turn out to be useless.

Forecasting the Future

The future of business process management lies in the hands of predictive analytics models and event processing. As you now know, predictive analytics is a methodology that applies special algorithms to data sets to create probability-based predictive models. These models anticipate or predict future activity.

Event processing, on the other hand, is a branch of computing that tracks streams of occurrences and searches for patterns in the data. Both of these are used with great success to forecast the future for businesses that want to reach the pinnacle of modern analytics and sales.

These systems allow businesses to quickly identify, meet, and anticipate customer needs in order to improve customer loyalty and revenue. Finding an appropriate business process management architecture that contains these predictive analytics systems is key to the future success of your company.

Pegasystems, for example, offers a unified BPM solution that combines business rules, process management, and analytics in one complete package. Predictive decisioning makes business process management more agile and proactive. This makes it far easier to take advantage of every single upsell or cross sell opportunity.

There is no doubt that predictive analytics is gaining traction in business. This technology uses the same data as business intelligence reports, but the insights are faster because of pre-set statistical models. New IT infrastructure that supports predictive analytics allows for rapid access to the data and super-fast calculations to occur.

If you want to increase the speed and automated decision capabilities of your business, then predictive analytics and quality rule engines are what you need. You can see why thought leaders are already calling predictive analytics the future of business intelligence.

When you can predict what your customer wants, you can sell them more products and services. This expands your revenue stream in a new way by capitalizing on existing customers instead of new customers.

Amazon.com, for example, has proven the cross and upsell

model of doing business, and they have applied this to millions of products across hundreds of categories. It's the reason that they are unmatched in the online world of ecommerce at this time.

Currently, predictive analytics is the only way to analyze and monitor past, present, and future customer behavior. In terms of business process management, forecasting the future is the only direction to move in from here. Implementing new business processes will be easier when you analyze your existing data in this new light.

It truly adds a third dimension onto the way you interact with your customer base. It is this customer-centric repositioning that will allow your company to sell in leaps and bounds in the future. Selecting the right tools for predictive analysis and business process management just became the most important decision your company has had to make in many years.

PART VI
Taking the Throne: Optimizing RTIM

CHAPTER 22
Interaction Assets

"There's a fundamental distinction between strategy and operational effectiveness."

MICHAEL PORTER

Back to the garden analogy—optimizing RTIM is like finding high quality business specimens that you would like to clone in other parts of your garden. You do not start from scratch; you begin with the best known solution and take it from there. It instills quality and evolutions into the business process. Making your best even better is going to be the standard business model a few years from now.

You are reaching the end stages of real time interaction management. All that is left to achieve is the optimization process. As you know, a system is only as good as its ability to improve itself over time. Your real time interaction management systems will need to be closely monitored and adjusted on a continuous basis.

Optimizing real time interactions means improving your operational intelligence and taking ownership of every individual customer interaction. You will know when your system begins to work because, nearly over night, the same customers you have had for years will begin to automatically start to drive toward accomplishing your strategic objectives. Whether it is buying more products and services from you or setting your company apart from the pack as a customer experience leader, when you plan, design, and implement intelligent interactions, the thought, planning, and execution start to prepay the business in the form of chunks of ROI benefit to your business.

Operational Intelligence and Real Time Insights to Project the Future

There are two things that every business needs if they are going to accurately predict the future: operational intelligence and real time customer insights. In reality, operational intelligence actually delivers these real time insights so that you can effectively predict the future. Once you can do this, the RTIM cycle begins.

This operational intelligence allows business users to take action in real time instead of missing opportunities for sales. Imagine if you could expose your customer to your best deals, marketing materials, and promotions when they are actually shopping for your products! It does not take a genius to know that sales would increase.

When corrective action can be taken during the transaction process, your business is automatically able to leverage individual opportunities as they happen. The real difference between operational intelligence and business intelligence is that OI provides real time, continuous analytics on past, present, and future streaming data.

Business intelligence only looks at historical data. You need to make the move from a state of business intelligence to a state of operational intelligence as they deliver the real time insights you will need to accurately predict the future of individual customer behaviors.

In other words, operational intelligence is designed to provide event driven analytics in real time while complementing the existing business intelligence data. No new data is introduced at the beginning; the system simply uses the old or existing data that it factors into its calculations. Then real time insights are created once the metrics are analyzed.

Projecting the future means that you will need real time big analytics data. This will allow your users to contrast, combine, and connect a large variety of data—hopefully onto a single dashboard for easy use. The architecture needs to be scalable so that it can dynamically move up or down depending on market demand.

A roadmap needs to be established so that the strategic plan for the platform, and each "garden" in the platform, can continually be improved. There are two levels of roadmap strategy owned and endorsed by each key leader and stakeholder. They need to have individual plans and process that come together to form the overall strategic plan in each "garden." Their accountability will result in accurate business process implementation as well as the correct customer interaction strategies that need to take place.

Creating an Ever Improving System

Operational intelligence is essentially the way your business uses methods and technologies to gain visibility into your own business to discover insights for IT, business, and analytics improvement. If you want an ever improving system, then you need to adopt and implement operational intelligence in your company.

- This intelligence allows your business to gain a deep understanding of itself by using relevant information sourced from machine data.
- It drastically reduces the time you need to detect important events.

- It reveals the most crucial patterns and analytics by drawing from multiple sources.
- It quickly deploys solutions that deliver the agility and flexibility needed.
- It leverages live feeds, historical data, and present data to understand what is happening. It will then identify problems and create solutions for you.

Business intelligence finds data sources that are structured, historical, and batch-loaded. Using ETL—or extract, transfer, and load—process, the structure is added into relational data bases. Operational intelligence is used with semi-structured and time series data. This data lets business users see what is happening now, and you can then compare it with what has happened long ago.

It bridges that questions gap and allows you to ask and answer questions that normal business intelligence systems cannot. But operational intelligence is not an alternative to business intelligence. They are actually highly complementary. With the right software and hardware on your side, you can easily transform your outdated BI system into a fully functional OI system.

To implement this ever improving system means that you will have to move from reactive to proactive methods. At the bottom of the roadmap lies search and investigation. Your IT department needs to understand that your machine data is a business asset. Proactive monitoring means that IT and business resources work together to find your problems in advance and learn how to present this machine data to the business in an actionable way.

Then, operational visibility needs to be considered. Your business becomes engaged with machine data analysis, and advanced models of behavior are created. Finally, real time business insights give way to dashboards, events, and predictive models that are used by your company to prevent problems and take advantage of opportunities.

Machines are creating data at an alarming rate. You can leverage this data to automate many of your real time interaction management systems. With operational intelligence on your side, you will find a way to keep your business data fresh, current, and usable when you need it. This system will continue to improve indefinitely because it has to.

Who Owns the Interaction?

It is true that we ALL own the interaction, but there really must be a "single throat to choke" when it comes to managing interactions. Chances are it will be a business process owner or a functional leader. Ideally, the COO or even the CEO would champion the effort, and then the business leaders would manage and be accountable for their "gardens."

Make sure that you know who the "owner" of the business garden is before you plant your interactions there. They will be very important in the near future and even more in the long run—as these individuals are the ones that are accountable overall for the interactions that you are optimizing.

A debate has risen about interactions and the customer experience. Who owns it? Is it sales or marketing or perhaps your customer service center? In order to better understand this often-asked question, you need to better understand the definition of an interaction.

Assuming that interactions are identical to customer experience, we can say that it is the perceptions that customers have across all of their interactions with your organization. This book is called *Intelligent Interactions* because YOU own them.

Everyone that is linked to your business owns your interactions. All of your employees, your project management teams, sponsors, and CEO—each of you has a different level of responsibility towards these interactions, but you own them as a collective.

A customer that deals with a nasty, impatient, and unhelpful front-end sales manager is going to judge their customer experience based on all of their past interactions with your company as well as this new unpleasant interaction. In the end, your brand is affected. You need to stop thinking in terms of silos and start thinking in terms of collaboration and mutual responsibility.

Your customers do not think in silos. They do not say, "Well, that sales team needs to sort out the attitude of that manager." Instead, they simply chalk it up to poor performance on the part of your entire company. Customers do not describe companies in terms of operational functionality or intelligence.

The question then changes slightly. If everyone owns the interaction, does that mean no one owns it? No! It means that top level management, like yourself, is directly responsible for every single interaction that is perpetrated under your brand name. The CEO and senior executives need to be customer centric first.

Once you have adopted real time interaction management, your cross functional teams will need to take care of the rest. But it begins with you. You are the owner of all interactions that come out of your business. When that sales manager fails, you fail. Customer experience and interactions are the most direct route to improving future sales.

You cannot finish this book and be satisfied that your business is currently doing the best it can for your customers. We both know that this simply is not true. You need to begin shaping and reforming your customer experience plans. This is the most direct route to doing that now and in the future.

Because you own these interactions, you also have the opportunity to improve them on a company-wide level. Creating a seamless and impressive customer experience is a delicate combination of good decisions, great technology, and impressive customer insights.

Monitoring and Improving Measurements

In operational intelligence, business activity monitoring is a capability that helps monitor business activities as they are applied to computer systems. The term refers to the aggregation, analysis, and presentation of real time information about activities on the inside of businesses that involve partners and customers.

These business activities are actually processes designed by business process management software. Why use business activity monitoring? It is the best way for front line as well as senior level management to review business activities. You will receive real time summaries that you can then draw insights from to measure and improve your business process management system.

These reports will contain real time information on transactional, operational, and process systems—detailing their current results and status for management to see. Using these reports, the "owners" of the business can make better decisions, take advantage of opportunities, and address problem areas as they arise.

Your business activity monitoring system will contain a dashboard that details your key performance indicators. You will use these to guarantee visibility across all of your activities and to improve performance over time.

These BAM systems, as they are called, can also automatically solve problems by correcting and restarting the previously failed process. There is always a high level of customization required for any business activity monitoring system.

It is possible to buy a template solution, but you will definitely need to hire a BAM expert in order to integrate it with your other systems. Otherwise, you can look at proposing an in-house build of your business activity monitoring system.

BAM is an essential part of operational intelligence as it provides visibility and awareness solutions to your business operations. It also helps you identify business problems, and you can change processes to increase business competitiveness by improving process efficiencies.

The core aim of business activity monitoring is to ensure that business goals remain related to revenue. For example, expenses, customer satisfaction, and profit expectations are all kept in line thanks to the continual reporting structure of a BAM system.

A BAM system is a great way to monitor your immediate business environment. All reports are done in real time, and they reflect the details of the decisions made and how the results have improved. There are dozens of ways to monitor your business or operational intelligence, but this is by far one of the most reliable methods.

Agile Cross Functional Governance

To understand agile cross functional governance means that you first have to understand agile governance as it relates to cross functional team dynamics. Agile governance is concerned with three main things: Are you building the right thing, building it properly, and building it in the designated time?

Traditional methods of corporate governance cannot keep up with the modern economy today. When you switch to Agile, you are making a decision to change the way you think, work, and interact. Agile corporate governance is actually a framework for the day-to-day management of organizations. Structurally, Agile governance deals with the Agile manager, integrated customer engagement, transparent and collaborative techniques, and continuous delivery.

A cross functional team, as you know, consists of experts collaborating across the entire software delivery cycle. People from IT, analytics, and the business departments are there, offering their expertise to the project as a whole. Everyone in this team is responsible for the delivery process.

To optimize real time interaction management, you literally have to plan for the harvest. Everyone has to work together to execute all of the activities associated with planning, executing, and delivering this harvest. It is important to implement Agile cross functional governance with YOU at the helm. When these two concepts are combined, the cross functional team becomes responsible for the Agile governance of your company.

Instead of a single project manager, CEO, or executive making all the decisions, the decisions are crowd-sourced by a dynamic team of experts from all the main departments of the company that have a vested interest in this capability being successful. Basically, it is an executive steering committee that feeds the cross functional governance team strategic direction and objectives.

The "everyone does everything" approach also means that your team members will be helping in areas where they do not have any expertise but have valuable knowledge to contribute for the improvement of the overall process.

This links back to the original cultural change that has to occur in your business. You will become involved in many pilot projects at the beginning phase—some that fail, others that succeed. The ones that succeed will give way to larger project teams that work on all kinds of strategic projects under this new governance model.

Self-service systems will rise, which means that automated changes occur, and anyone in the team can deploy changes to their garden or operational environment. Your end customer becomes the actual user as you take advantage of insanely fast feedback loops.

A cross functional team working on an Agile project is ideal for ongoing improvements across a wide variety of operations. Many responsibilities need to be shared in teams that want to succeed with Agile project management.

You will need to develop an Agile environment within your company first before proposing cross functional teams. Otherwise, there may be some confusion or reluctance to this new system. It demands that your designers, for example, do more than just design—and some employees could have a real problem with this.

CHAPTER 23
Best Practices for Optimization

"We must develop knowledge optimization initiatives to leverage our key learnings."

SCOTT ADAMS

There are best practices in optimization that concern technology and strategy and the eventual outcome of your decision management systems. These are discussed in this chapter and should give you a better sense of where to focus when optimizing your real time interaction management systems.

- Road map (outline) business interactions leveraging a test and learn environment.

The platform roadmap should detail one-, three-, and five-year accomplishments that the business is actively working toward. Leader roadmaps will have similar, if not identical, timeframes. The key measure of success depends on the key leaders that have set RTIM into their team strategies and are allocating present and future resources to this capability.

Workbenches for Predictive Analytics

Predictive analytics workbenches are a set of software components that have been created to analyze data sources to find out what the mathematical relationships are in data that will produce a predictive analytics model that represents those relationships.

A workbench of this nature will target an analyst or someone that knows a fair amount about predictive analytics as a whole. This analyst will also understand the data that the organization analyzes and the business needs that must be met. In other words, a predictive analytics workbench targets someone that has a firm grasp on all core departments, underlying data, and operational needs for each department.

The goal of predictive analytics workbenches is to outline a set of business capabilities that allows users to actively perform important tasks for the business. Some of these tasks are to prepare data for modeling, to build predictive and statistical models, to manage deployed models, to connect to data, to assess the business impact of these models, and to visualize the data.

These predictive analytics workbenches support a lot of different modeling processes, including clustering, decision trees, rule induction, linear regression, K-means, affinity analysis, genetic algorithms, nearest neighbor, neural networks, and logistic regression. These are then used to build four main classes of models:

- *Statistical models:* These are used to validate a hypothesis
- *Clustering models:* Group similar data sets together to create ways of looking at profiles of each cluster. These models are used to gain a broader understanding of a customer base.
- *Association models:* These models find situations in the data where events have happened and there is a good chance they will happen again. They are used most often in analyzing customer basket data and for recommendation engines on shopping sites.

- **Predictive analytic models:** Patterns and trends are looked for in this model, and the data provides a predicted outcome. The results could be binary or numeric—or multiple results based.

At any one time the analyst could have access to more than 20 different algorithms, though none of these are guaranteed to be the best in any particular situation. Models will be built and scored to see if they have the highest profit, accuracy, or return on investment.

The workbench itself is where the analyst will create, validate, manage, and deploy different predictive models. They consist of a number of components, namely a model repository, data visualization and analysis tools, deployment tools, design tools, modeling algorithms, and data management tools.

Basically, the analyst will use design tools, data management, modeling algorithms, and data visualization and analysis in the model repository. It will be deployed as a decision service in an executable model, which will be added to the operational database. Then it will be applied to the product and tested.

Interaction Assets: Doing More With Less

Real time interaction management systems are huge assets for your business as are the data and decision capabilities that continue to improve. These interaction assets allow you to do more with less, resulting in widespread and continuous garden growth.

As you learn more about interactions, you will come to treat them as assets. It is like constructing business "Legos" that you can clone and put into other areas of your business to drive consistency across interaction channels.

Data collection and analysis in loyalty program relationships give marketers an edge in real time marketing. With better insight into their behaviors, they are more likely to influence a customer to buy at the right moment. But analytics and data do not replace judgment. With data, learning and accurate decision making must be adhered to in order to optimize the process. This is what "right time" marketing is all about.

A few years ago all senior executives would talk about was finding a way to reduce operating costs without compromising customer service quality. Real time interactions allow you to reduce operating costs while you steadily *improve* your customer service quality!

Here is how you are going to do more with less in the coming year:

- *Modernization:* When you modernize your systems, everything improves. Enjoy business process management that uses decision management systems, predictive analytics, and rule engines to keep your business current—forever.
- *Automation:* These great real time interaction management systems allow you to automate key processes that are dynamic, collaborative, and unstructured. Enjoy guided interactions that work for you automatically as part of your modern system.
- *Innovation:* You will be able to innovate more as your real time interaction management systems continually update and improve over time. This means you will not miss any opportunities to improve your service delivery, and your customers will continue to buy, inflating your revenue.
- *Customer-centricity:* Your business will be more customer-centric, which is the very definition of doing more with less. With just your new RTIM system, you can achieve incredible things with your customer retention and service delivery. You will always know the "next best action" to take to get individual customers to buy in both the short and long term.
- *Real time process management (Six Sigma) approach:* It is your business objective to improve quality and reduce variation by

ensuring that critical to quality (CTQ) measures are mapped and automated in your business process management solution. With your interaction assets, you keep these processes under control, doing more with less.

It is fairly common that businesses have a tight window to introduce new and innovative services to their service profile. By automating these dynamic cases, you really reduce the effort needed to get new processes from the idea phase to the implementation phase.

Time is also greatly sped up with real time interaction management systems. Because there are no longer silo barriers but collaborative teams, decisions are more accurate and diverse, and there is better communication, which makes for speedier decision making.

Guided customer interactions help your customers achieve their objectives in a smooth, customized manner. With Lean, you can get rid of wasteful processes and increase your process creation speed. It all contributes to a more efficient business process management solution.

Experimenting With Processes

Your business processes are really what make your business great, so it is important to continually experiment with them so that improvements can occur as time rolls by. Remember that a business process is a set of activities that represents steps that need to be taken to achieve a certain objective.

But there are perhaps thousands of different ways you can get from A to B in business. Knowing what your end goal is going to be is the first step. From there, you can continue to add, remove, or streamline steps in your process until an ideal situation seems to present itself. Eventually, enough time will go by, and it will be updated again.

Using your process maps, your teams will be able to adjust or integrate new ideas on a micro level into your standing business processes. It may come to your attention that your supply system has a very obvious fault that always causes delays. While real time interaction management systems will identify and potentially correct this fault, it will also continue to ensure that your existing process is the best version it can be.

Experimentation is a vital optimization tool to use when working with business process management. Within this experimentation, you can use modeling and simulation to manage change in your systems. Simulation clearly outlines the reasons for change without actually having to implement a whole new system first.

Simulation also shows you HOW you arrived at your answer as well as cause and effect, and you will be able to generate explanations for the decisions you make. As part of a business rule engine, simulation is an offline solution to newly designed processes.

Along with simulation, you will be able to use exceptional organizational improvement methodologies like Six Sigma. Then you can define, measure, analyze, and improve the participation of everyone involved so that quality is neatly managed. With the right controls in place, simulation is an essential tool in change management.

There are many different kinds of simulation models. They can represent a large range of business capabilities and need to reproduce or project the behavior of a modeled system. These PC-based simulations can be simple or very complex.

The four main kinds of simulation modeling are: a system of interest, like a meta model; a management system; a physical system; or a visibility system, transparent or black-box-like. A probability model can be deterministic or probabilistic. Finally, a dynamic model can be either dynamic or steady-state.

Whatever simulation model you choose to use, know this. The more your company runs these experiments and model simulations, the faster your systems will improve. That means faster and better customer experiences for your company. This is directly in line with your end goal of gaining more profit.

How Technology Enables the System

There are certain "enablers" that help real time interaction management systems work. Technology is by far the most potent of these enablers. There are a wide range of technologies that can enable the development of real time interaction management systems in your organization.

Core technologies like predictive analytics, optimization systems, and business rule management systems lie at the heart of these enabling technologies. Together, these allow for a number of significant benefits that your organization will experience.

- *Decreased data latency:* Business intelligence apps usually have some form of data latency. It might take a minute or so to process a complex data query. The correct information systems technology can completely eliminate data latency, allowing you to access the most current data in real time.

- *Decreased time latency:* In the past, it was common for organizations to have to update their systems on a daily or weekly basis. Sometimes these systems would automatically update overnight. The right technology now does this in real time, which means that you will never use outdated data in important decision-making systems.

- *Business activity monitoring:* You will be able to analyze data in real time instantly thanks to your BAM solution that collects and processes it in real time from a large variety of sources. Your senior management will benefit from these business activity reports as they will be able to make essential decisions based on current data results.

Real time analysis of rapidly changing operational data is really how technology enables a real time interaction management system. To achieve intelligent interactions, the right software and hardware must be chosen and integrated into your existing systems.

The wrong software could impede your goals or, worse, disrupt the customer experience improvement cycle. Technology is the one thing that guarantees your systems will be better six months from the day you implement them. This continuous improvement cycle will become more important as markets shrink and competition grows.

Your business rules management system contains all the software components you need to test, create, manage, deploy, and maintain the business rules that govern an operational environment. With this system, you will be able to link business rules to data sources and identify conflicts and quality problems in a way that makes you more money now and in the future.

Enabling the system means helping every process achieve its goal. The best technology platforms will help your real time interaction management systems reduce costs, improve customer retention and service, reduce risk and errors, and rapidly improve revenue across the entire company.

Your Data Infrastructure

You already know that decision management systems cannot function without data. It forms the basis for all quality predictive analytic models used by decision management systems. These systems must be integrated with data infrastructure so that when a decision needs to be made, the right recommended information is delivered.

This information on how decisions are made need to be stored so that your teams can assess and analyze it later on. There are five parts of data infrastructure that are particularly important for decision management systems.

- ***Data Warehouses:*** Your organization will have an enterprise data warehouse, or several localized warehouses, to complement your operational databases. These will contain multiple organizational silos. The data stored here is well integrated and easier to use for the company.

- **Operational Databases:** These contain raw and transactional data used to build predictive analytic models that need to be used when decisions are made. While these operational databases support the transaction element, decision management systems need the same access to this transactional data.
- **Analytic Data Marts:** When data is extracted from operational databases or data warehouses, often analytics data marts are made. A single business unit will own it, and it will allow this group more flexibility and control with the data they need. In most cases, spreadsheet access, online analytical processing, and reporting are the reasons to creation these analytic data marts.
- **Big Data Platforms:** It is now affordable to gather and analyze large volumes of data in terabytes or petabytes. This data is often stored in semi-structured relational databases. Network traffic, data from sensors and devices, log data from apps and document, and video and text data are all included here.
- **In-Database Analytics:** Many organizations offer predictive analytic modeling that is built into an existing database. These "in-database" analytics allow for models to be created and scored without extracting any data from the database. This improves performance and allows for execution to occur on the data hardware instead of the analytic server hardware.

The rule is generally that more data is better, though this can be untrue in certain situations. A flood of data can cause analysis paralysis, which in turn will lead to over-engineered rules that do not quite focus on the issues that result in core success. Keep this in mind when setting up your data infrastructure.

In these new big data systems, the analytic capabilities are steadily evolving. The problem here is that tools have not developed this much just yet, and they have a long way to go to reach the same ease-of-use as traditional tools in analytics.

Pre-Configured or Automated RTIM Systems

To adequately optimize your real time interaction management system, you will need to pre-configure and automate as much as you can. Companies that decide to use the decision management approach often do it because they are facing a specific problem.

This business problem can be solved because it can be quantified. Key measurements are put in place to ensure that the issue has been addressed and resolved. A process like this makes it easier for organizations to justify investing in real time interaction management systems like these.

Pre-configured decision management systems are usually focused on companies like these as they require a set solution to implement instead of a custom solution. Software as a service (SaaS) solutions are an option in this case, or there are add-ons that you can buy.

These set solutions are a combination of predictive analytics, business rules, and optimization that have be packaged as a single application for instant use.

Pre-configured decision management systems can address many of the following concerns: inbound and outbound marketing, debt collection, price optimization, credit risk, targeted direct marketing, next best offer, insurance and healthcare fraud, and retail planning or merchandising.

These automated pre-configured decision services can be used by your company instead of the formulaic business rules management system, predictive analytics workbench, and optimization system. There are different pros and cons as you would expect.

Some of the pros to using these automated solutions include using one integrated user interface that your employees will use to create and maintain your decision service. It is far simpler when the service focuses on one business problem, and there are lower IT requirements because of the all-<u>on</u>-one solution.

A cloud-based software as a service option means that it is a very controlled environment with less management needed and less IT overhead. The content is delivered with pre-built reports and models so deployment is super-fast. Finally, it is easier to deploy updates with these set systems, and it causes IT, business, and analytics teams to rally around a single issue.

The cons, on the other hand, mean that you will have limited cross-silo learning, which means that even though you can focus decision management systems on one area successfully, the greater benefits of implementing this on a company-wide scale may be lost. These set systems also tend to integrate poorly with existing business rules and predictive analytics systems.

Finally, there are fewer options outside of fraud and marketing—meaning that if you have an issue that does not relate to either of these, then you will struggle to find an appropriate package solution. There is just less flexibility with these systems, especially when you try to use them for a problem they were not intended for.

Being a Service Orientated Platform

Another best practice is for decision management systems to be built and deployed in a certain architectural framework. Decision management systems are often used to modernize legacy applications—with the decision service deployed to a mainframe. They can also be deployed to control equipment or kiosks or imbedded in machinery.

Many of these are deployed using an SOA infrastructure, or Service Orientated Architecture. They are then coupled with business process management systems and event processing systems. Sometimes only one is integrated with the SOA.

When you use an SOA, you break up system functionality into

a number of services that work together to provide the level of functionality required. All elements have defined interfaces that make it reliable for other services. Often these interfaces hide details of the implementation, which means that services can be created following a unique design approach or be in a different language yet they work together.

You already know that the core of a decision management system is the decision service. This service answers decision-making questions for the many other services. While they do not need to be rolled out as a service, they can be added to a mainframe module or a software component. SOA works very well for decision services.

A business process management system allows all necessary tasks to be defined and executed according to the needs of the business. They can involve multiple systems integration, data entry, human reviews, and automated tasks. Decision management systems often include integration with business processes that are used to determine which transactions need to be reviewed.

The software components that aid business process management systems include monitoring and reporting on process execution, integrating many systems into a single process flow, defining and managing the business process tasks, and executing system and human tasks to achieve the desired business outcome or result.

Event processing systems, on the other hand, allow for the collection of events from any source over any timeframe so that the right action can be taken. Event processing gathers clouds of events and evaluates them to formulate the desired response. These systems are often used with decision management systems. The event processing system will ask the right question, and the decision management system will provide the right answer.

These event systems enrich live data with information from the business, and they capture live data from various sources. They aid in triggering action on patterns that are detected and assist tools in allowing business users to handle the changing environment by modifying existing action logic and patterns in a reliable way.

Conclusion

Real time interaction management systems are not only the future; they are the most direct route to expanding your company profits without having to seek out new customers from an over stimulated and flooded global market.

I hope that this book has shown you how important it is to take action and implement your own decision management systems. I also hope that you have gotten enough practical information to create intelligent interactions that will keep your organization moving forward for many years to come. When in doubt, keep your eye on the money! These systems can produce an enormous amount of benefits with relatively small shifts. Use a proven approach—TIPP—to "hedge your bets" on RTIM. You can really mess these implementations up if you neglect any components of the TIPP approach

These are proven technology systems that radically revamp the way that you do business. It is time for a customer-centric approach that allows you to reach new levels in business performance. To fully maximize operational efficiency, you will need to create, implement, and manage these revolutionary systems into your business now.

Many organizations have decision management systems, but few use them in the correct manner. There are even more businesses out there that are still focused on securing new customers at the cost of neglecting current customers. That is a huge example of "leaving money on the table."

Do not be one of these ailing businesses. Customers do not have time for companies that do not keep up with their needs. You need to unify your IT, analytics, and business departments and introduce them to this new way of expanding your reach, improving customer experience, and increasing overall sales.

When you understand what the individual customer wants, it becomes a simple matter of interacting with them at the right time with the right intelligence. Real time interaction management systems give you the power to understand the changing behaviors of your core customer base so that you can leverage it for profit.

The opportunity here is right in front of you. Your agile, flexible, and data-based decision management system will forge a new path for your company in the future. All you have to do is discover and model the decisions you will need. Then you have to design and implement these decisions as decision services. Finally, create the process and infrastructure you need to continually improve how your decisions are made.

Combine this decision management system with the correct business rules and optimization, and you have a real time interaction management system that will grow with your company. It will make you progressively stronger in a niche field that has turned thousands into millions and millions into billions.

You have to focus on getting the TIPP approach to real time interaction management into your business right now. Time waits for no man and certainly no business. While you consider all the extra effort that implementing a system like this will take, consider how far ahead you will be in front of your competition with this new capability.

TIPP—the competitive advantage done your way. Setting this capability up correctly is more than half the battle. Anyone can write a check and buy software...but making money and achieving ROI...now that is what TIPP is all about!

References

Vittal, Suresh, *Interaction Optimizer,* http://www.portraitsoftware.com/sites/portrait/files/media/pdf/brochures/InteractionOptimizer_Brochure.pdf

Hadley, Ed, *Real Time Interaction Management: 9 Alternatives To Pure Offers,* http://blog.neolane.com/real-time-marketing/interaction-management/

Business Process Management, Wikipedia

http://en.wikipedia.org/wiki/Business_process_management

Zaibak, Omar, *99 Legendary Customer Service Quotes,* http://www.customer1.com/blog/customer-service-quotes

Change Management Frequently Asked Questions Tutorial, http://www.change-management.com/tutorial-FAQ.htm

Washington, Marvin, Hacker, Stephen, Hacker, Marla, Successful Organizational Transformation, *What Is a Burning Platform?,* http://my.safaribooksonline.com/book/-/9781606492116/chapter-9dot-the-burning-platform/what_is_a_burning_platform

Resource Wall of Fire, http://www.mentoric.com/resource_wall_of_fire.html

Customer Content Management, https://www.icdp.net/how-can-we-help-you/customer-insight/customer-contact-management.aspx

Functional Silo, http://www.technology-training.co.uk/functionalsilo.php

Gulati, Ranjay, Prof, *The Four Cs Of Customer-Focused Solutions,* Harvard Business School Publishing Corporation, http://hbr.org/web/special-collections/insight/customers/silo-busting-how-to-execute-on-the-promise-of-customer-focus

How Functional Silos Can Kill The Customer Experience And 3 Steps To Avoid Catastrophie, http://jlwatsonconsulting.typepad.com/my-blog/2011/08/how-functional-silos-can-kill-the-customer-experience-and-3-steps-to-prevent-death.html

Selling Across Cultures – Increase Profit And Customer Loyalty, Communicaid Group Ltd 2010, http://www.communicaid.com/cross-cultural-training/blog/cross-cultural-training/selling-across-cultures-%E2%80%93-increase-profit-and-customer-loyalty/

Garrity, Chris, *A Corporate Culture Of Customer Loyalty,* http://ctsmithiii.wordpress.com/2012/05/04/a-corporate-culture-of-customer-loyalty/

How Southwest Airlines Built a Culture of Customer Loyalty, http://www.slideshare.net/parature/how-southwest-airlines-built-a-culture-of-customer-loyalty

Cheng. Larry, *On The Blind Men And An Elephant,* http://larrycheng.com/2010/01/23/on-the-blind-men-and-an-elephant/

Business Analytics: Uncommon Insights, http://www.deloitte.com/view/en_US/us/Services/additional-services/deloitte-analytics-service/417b6aa842309210VgnVCM200000bb42f00aRCRD.htm

Mintzberg's 5Ps Of Strategy: Developing A better strategy, http://www.mindtools.com/pages/article/mintzberg-5ps.htm

The functional Level Of Culture, http://www.tmcorp.com/Perspectives/Articles/The-Functional-Level-of-Culture/118/

Horizon Issue: Rising Customer Expectations, http://www.op.nysed.gov/reports/rising_consumer_expectations.pdf

Focus On Rising Customer Expectations, http://disruptivemedia.se/focus-rising-customer-expectations

Uzor, Ben, Jr, *Online Shopping Fuels Rise In Customer Expectations, Cisco Study,* http://businessdayonline.com/NG/index.php/tech/78-computing/40131-online-shopping-fuels-rise-in-customer-expectations-cisco-study

Zaibak, Omar, *99 Legendary Customer Service Quotes,* http://www.customer1.com/blog/customer-service-quotes

Economist Intelligence Unit, *The Burning Platform*, http://www.slideshare.net/Management-Thinking/the-burning-platform-how-companies-are-managing-change-in-a-recession

Chapter 4

BI Quotes To Remember, https://sites.google.com/site/fsubiwiki/home/bi-quotes-to-remember

Zaman, M, *Predictive Analytics: The Future of Business Intelligence*, www.mahmoudyoussef.com/BI/9.doc

Data Quality, Lingaro, http://www.lingaro.com/?q=node/27

What Is Business Intelligence?, http://charc-concepts.org/what-is-business-intelligence/

Predictive Analytics, Wikipedia, http://en.wikipedia.org/wiki/Predictive_analytics#Predictive_models

Gualtieri, Mike, *The Forrester Wave: Big Data Predictive Analytics Solutions, Q1 2013*, http://www.forrester.com/pimages/rws/reprints/document/85601/oid/1-LTEQDI

Understanding Predictive Analytics, Fico, http://www.fico.com/en/Communities/PredictiveAnalytics/Pages/what-are-the-main-types-of-predictive-analytics.aspx

What Are The Types of Predictive Analytics?, Fico, http://dmblog.fico.com/2006/06/what_are_the_ty.html

Gottesdiener, Ellen, *Business Rules*, http://www.busanalysiselearning.com/Pubs/Articles/BusinessRulesShowPowerPromise-Gottesdiener.pdf

Berk, *Evaluating Predicative Models*, http://www.stat.cmu.edu/~cshalizi/350/lectures/19/lecture-19.pdf

Collins, Sam, *The Power of Business Rules – The Jungle Gym of Customer Service*, http://www.callcentreclinic.com/news/the-power-of-business-rules--the-jungle-gym-of-customer-service-47961.htm

Predictive Modeling Technology, http://www.predx.com/docs/PredxModelingTechnology.pdf

Taylor, James, *The Power of Business Rules Management*, http://www.information-management.com/news/the-power-of-business-rules-management-10023735-1.html?zkPrintable=1&nopagination=1

Chapter 5

Leadership Quotes, http://www.notable-quotes.com/l/leadership_quotes.html

Capability Management in Business, http://en.wikipedia.org/wiki/Capability_management_in_business

Decision Management Systems Platform Capabilities, http://decisionmanagementsolutions.com/decision-management-technology#capabilities

Schafferling, Andre, Wagner, Heinz-Theo, Becker, Jochen, *Exploring The Relation Between Firm Ownership and IT Capability,* http://aisel.aisnet.org/ecis2012/6/

IT Business Capability Planning Objectives, http://www.it101forbusiness.com/managing-it-as-a-business/it-business-capability-planning-objectives/

NICE Customer Interaction Management Solutions, http://www.nice.com/enterprise-solutions

Vroom, Victor, Searle, John, G, *Educating Managers For Decision Making and Leadership,* http://www.hr-meter.com/files/vroomartikelfuerweb.pdf

Chapter 6

Rouse, Margaret, *Interaction Management,* http://searchsoa.techtarget.com/definition/interaction-management

Weber, Stacey, *Enabling Cross-Functional Teams: A Leadership Role For Product Managers,* http://www.pragmaticmarketing.com/resources/enabling-cross-functional-teams-a-leadership-role-for-product-managers

Zoerman, Kristofer, W, *Cross-Functional Efficiency,* http://www.zoerman.com/cfe.pdf

Meyer, Dumaine, Parker, *Key Guidelines For Managing Cross Functionality,* http://www.humancapitalreview.org/content/default.asp?Article_ID=945

Hadley, Ed, *Real-Time Interaction Management: 9 Alternatives To Pure Offers,* http://blog.neolane.com/real-time-marketing/interaction-management/

Buyens, Marc, *The Case For Business Interaction Management (BIM)*, http://www.xpragma.com/bim_wp.php

Hinchcliffe, Dion, *Dion Hinchcliffe's Next Generation Enterprises*, http://www.ebizq.net/blogs/enterprise/2009/11/eight_reasons_why_data-centric.php

Carole-Ann, *A Practical Guide To Business Objectives and KPI's*, http://techondec.wordpress.com/

Peterson, Rob, *12 Experts Define Key Performance Indicators (KPI's)*, http://barnraisersllc.com/2012/02/experts-define-key-performance-indicators/

Williamson, Robert, *What Gets Measured Gets Done*, http://www.swspitcrew.com/articles/What%20Gets%20Measured%201106.pdf

Slater, Jeff, *What Get Measured Gets Done*, http://www.isixsigma.com/community/blogs/what-gets-measured-gets-done/

Decision Management Systems Platform Capabilities, http://decisionmanagementsolutions.com/decision-management-technology#capabilities

A Business Guide To IT Capability Planning, http://www.it101forbusiness.com/managing-it-as-a-business/it-business-capability-planning-objectives/

Chapter 7

Sanchez, Tim, *22 Inspirational Customer Service Quotes*, http://deliverbliss.com/inspirational-customer-service-quotes

Burns, Megan, Manning, Harley, Peterson, Jennifer, Catino, Shelby, *The Business Impact of Customer Experience, 2010*, http://www.forrester.com/The+Business+Impact+Of+Customer+Experience+2010/fulltext/-/E-RES57617?objectid=RES57617

Customer Engagement Strategies, http://www.customerengagement.com/next/Four%20Stages%20of%20Customer%20Interaction.pdf

Barnes, Hank, *Prioritizing and Measuring Customer Experience Projects*, http://www.customerthink.com/blog/prioritizing_and_measuring_customer_experience_projects

Forlizzi, Jodi, Zimmerman, John, Mancuso, Vince, Kwak, Sonya, *How Interface Agents Affect Interaction Between Humans and Computers*, http://goodgestreet.com/docs/Forlizzi_DPPI07.pdf

Coiera, Enrico, *Mediated Agent Interaction*, http://www3.chi.unsw.edu.au/pubs/aime-01-mediated%20agent%20interaction.pdf

Software Agent, Wikipedia, http://en.wikipedia.org/wiki/Software_agent

Prioritizing Projects To Maximize Return on Investment, http://www.ccpace.com/resources/documents/maximizeROI_whitepaper.pdf

ROI Decisions.com, http://roidecisions.wordpress.com/2013/01/22/roi-decisons-com-a-good-decision-is-always-driving-r-o-i/

Gragg, Bart, *Strategic Vs. Tactical Decisions – Returns on Investment (ROI) in Writing a Business Plan (pt. 3)*, http://www.bluecollaru.com/strategic-vs-tactical-decisions-return-on-investmentroi-in-writing-a-business-plan-pt-3/

Chapter 8

Expectations Quotes, http://www.brainyquote.com/quotes/keywords/expectations.html

Role of Executive Sponsors When Managing Change, http://www.change-management.com/sponsor-roles.htm

Project Roles and Responsibilities, http://www2.cit.cornell.edu/computer/robohelp/cpmm/Project_Roles_and_Responsibilities.htm

Taylor, James, *Critical Questions For Decision Management: Value Architecture Ownership*, https://www-950.ibm.com/events/wwe/grp/grp004.nsf/vLookupPDFs/James%20Taylor%20-%20Critical%20Questions%20DecisionManagement%20-%20IBM%20Napa%20Summit%202012/$file/James%20Taylor%20-%20Critical%20Questions%20DecisionManagement%20-%20IBM%20Napa%20Summit%202012.pdf

Taylor, James, *Business Decision Management Part 2*, http://www.bpminstitute.org/resources/articles/business-decision-management-part-2

Decision Management Technology, http://decisionmanagementsolutions.com/decision-management-technology

Taylor, James, *Next Generation Claims Systems With Decision Management*, http://www.decisionmanagementsolutions.com/attachments/159_Next%20Generation%20Claims%20with%20Decision%20Management.pdf

Executive Sponsor, Wikipedia, http://en.wikipedia.org/wiki/Executive_sponsor

Taylor, James, *Cloud Based Predictive Analytics Poised For Rapid Growth*, http://decisionmanagementsolutions.com/attachments/article/192/CloudPredictiveAnalyticsPoisedForGrowthFinal.pdf

Hood, James, *Decision Management in Programs and Agile Projects*, http://projectmanager.com.au/beyond-projects/program-management/decision-management-in-programs-and-agile-projects/

Agile Project Management, http://www.tutorialspoint.com/management_concepts/agile_project_management.htm

PMBOK Vs. PRINCE2 Vs. Agile Project Management, http://www.cio.com.au/article/402347/pmbok_vs_prince2_vs_agile_project_management/

Chapter 9

Designing For Interaction Quotes, http://www.goodreads.com/work/quotes/5972-designing-for-interaction-creating-smart-applications-and-clever-device

Salaski, Patrick, *Capability Maturity Assessment*, http://www.trissential.com/PDF/Training-WOrkshops/TCBAF/2013/01-15-2013/TCBAF_Presentation_01-15-2013.pdf

Mango, Bob, *To Build Vs. To Buy: Comparing Custom and Off-Shelf Software Applications*, http://www.3csoftware.com/resources/articles/to-build-or-to-buy-comparing-custom-and-off-the-shelf-software-applications/

Machigad, Vijay, *Offshore Models For Engineering Product Development*, http://www.infosys.com/engineering-services/lifecycle-management/white-papers/documents/captive-vendor-partner.pdf

Best Practices in Decision Management Systems, http://decisionmanagementsolutions.com/decision-management-technology#best-practices

Ledeen, Kenneth, *A Decision Paradigm For Information Technology*

Applications, http://www.nevo.com/our-knowledge/whitepapers/BuildVsBuy.pdf

Murthi, Sanjay, *Build Versus Buy-Making The Right Decision,* http://www.developer.com/java/other/article.php/1488331/Build-Versus-BuymdashMaking-the-Right-Decision.htm

Oliver, Dan, *Buy Vs. Build: Six Steps To making The Right Decision,* http://www.techrepublic.com/article/buy-vs-build-six-steps-to-making-the-right-decision/1038857

12 Questions To Assess Your Company's Capability For Breakthrough Innovation, http://www.grabbinglightning.com/12-questions-to-assess-your-companys-capability-for-breakthrough-innovation/

Suda, Brian, *The Design Choices You Make For Information: How To Create Great Data Visualizations,* http://www.uie.com/events/virtual_seminars/how_to_info_design/

Singer, Natasha, *When The Data Struts Its Stuff,* http://www.nytimes.com/2011/04/03/business/03stream.html?_r=0

Customer Engagement Strategies, http://www.customerengagement.com/next/Four%20Stages%20of%20Customer%20Interaction.pdf

Chapter 10

Business Quotes, http://www.businessperformancemanagement.info/business-quotes.html/

Jaako, Leah, *Inside The Mind of a Fashionista: The What and Why Of Purchase Choices,* http://www.visioncritical.com/blog/customer-insights-with-business-intelligence

Applied Customer Insight, http://www.logica.com/we-do/applied-customer-insight/

Davis, Judith, *Right-Time Business Intelligence: Optimizing The Business Decision Cycle,* http://www.cwrld.net/pdfs/sybase_free_realtime_wp.pdf

Business Intelligence (BI) How To Build Successful BI Strategy, http://www.deloitte.com/assets/DcomSouthAfrica/Local%20Assets/Documents/Business%20intelligence%20that%20aligns%20with%20enterprise%20goals.pdf

Peacock, Marisa, *Aprimo Manages Multi-Channel Marketing in Real Time*, http://www.cmswire.com/cms/customer-experience/aprimo-manages-multichannel-marketing-in-real-time-012379.php

Part 8: Real Time Business Information Solutions For Gravic, http://www.gravic.com/shadowbase/uses/real-timesolutionsfromgravic.html

Real-Time Business Intelligence: Instant Opportunities, Hitachi Data Systems, http://www.hds.com/assets/pdf/hitachi-unified-compute-platform-for-sap-hana-white-paper.pdf

Chapter 11

Jacko, Peter, *Incentive Alignment in Corporations*, http://www.strom.sk/~pj/works/incentive.pdf

Hoffman, Jody, Rogelberg, Steven, *A Guide To Team Incentive Systems*, http://orgscience.uncc.edu/sites/orgscience.uncc.edu/files/understanding%20team%20incentive%20systems.pdf

Understanding Communication Channels, http://homepages.wmich.edu/~bowman/channels.html

Miller, Janice, Osinkski, Diana, *Training Needs Assessment*, http://www.ispi.org/pdf/suggestedReading/Miller_Osinski.pdf

Training and Development, https://www.opm.gov/policy-data-oversight/training-and-development/planning-evaluating/

Rodriguez, Juan, *What Is An Environmental Assessment?*, http://construction.about.com/od/Construction-Management/a/What-Is-An-Environmental-Assessment.htm

Chapter 12

BPM Quotes of The Week, http://adamdeane.wordpress.com/2012/10/13/bpm-quotes-112/

Customer Experience Makeover, Rightnow, http://www.rightnow.com/files/whitepapers/Customer_Experience_Makeover__A_Practical_Approach_to_Differentiated_Service.pdf

An Architecture For Differentiated Services, http://www.hjp.at/doc/rfc/rfc2475.html#sec_2

Differentiated Services, Wikipedia, http://en.wikipedia.org/wiki/Differentiated_services

Building a Differentiated Service Experience Strategy, http://www.accenture.com/SiteCollectionDocuments/PDF/Accenture-Building-Differentiated-Service-Experience-Strategy.pdf

Differentiated Services, http://www.cisco.com/en/US/products/ps6610/products_ios_protocol_group_home.html

Khoshafian, Setrag, *Real Time Six Sigma With PegaRULEs Process Commander*

Chapter 13

Technology Quotes, http://www.brainyquote.com/quotes/topics/topic_technology.html

Decision Management Deployment, http://www.statanalytics.com/deployment.php

Real-Time Interaction Management, http://www.information-management.com/infodirect/20000317/2034-1.html

Predictive Customer Interaction Management, http://www.tibco.com/multimedia/wp-predictive-customer-interaction-management_tcm8-2462.pdf

Taylor, James, *Decision Management Systems,* Page 1-255

Chapter 14

Dresner, Howard, *Six Recommendations For Implementing Business Intelligence Solutions,* http://sandhill.com/article/six-recommendations-for-implementing-business-intelligence-solutions/

Dynamic Testing, Wikipedia, http://en.wikipedia.org/wiki/Dynamic_testing

Adventures With Testing BI/DW Application: On a Crusade To Find The Holy Grail, http://msdn.microsoft.com/en-us/library/gg248101.aspx

Bajaj, Nikhil, *BI Testing,* http://api.ning.com/files/myiaUX8SMcBkLpJVgz09KymaNcCTIvLgciHjHwqYGVCyRpqNG6igsQalkTo-cGVI9kkgDq-v2qvWqqsaBCza5gbrGXNFzahj/BI_testing_tutorial_V1.0.pdf

SAS Business Intelligence – A Perceptive Vision In Clinical Trials, http://info.quanticate.com/bid/93261/SAS-Business-Intelligence-A-Perceptive-Vision-in-Clinical-Trials

Willmor, David, Embury, Suzanne, *Testing The Implementation of Business Rules using Intentional Database Tests,* http://www.cs.man.ac.uk/~willmord/files/WillmorEmbury-TAICPART06.pdf

Business Rule Engine Implementation, http://hexaware.com/business-rule-engine-implementation.htm

Business Intelligence Implementation, http://mosaic.arizona.edu/files/files/BI_3-2-09.pdf

Operational Intelligence – Informed Decisions Daily, http://www.entsgo.com/Content/Operations/OperationalIntelligence.pdf

Figueira, Adam, *Strategies For Successful Testing: Optimizing Conversion Rates With Real Time Intelligence,* http://monetate.com/2011/11/strategies-for-successful-testing-real-time-intelligence-and-decision-making/

Chapter 15

20 Awesome Quotes On Change Management, http://www.torbenrick.eu/blog/change-management/20-awesome-quotes-on-change-management/

Proactive Compliance For Consumer Protection, http://www.nice.com/proactive-compliance-consumer-protection

Caddell, John, *Agent Performance Vs. Compliance: How Interaction Analytics Keeps The Scales Balanced,* http://blog.nexidia.com/agentperformance-vs-compliance/

Caddell, John, *Compliance Series #3 – An Operationalized Compliance management System,* http://blog.nexidia.com/tagcompliance-seriesan-operationalized-compliance-management-system/

Nickols, Fred, *Change Management 101,* http://www.nickols.us/change.pdf

Change Management 101: An Executive Guide To Change Management, http://www.cio.com.au/article/268210/change_management_101_an_executive_guide_change_management/

Change Management Communication Planning, http://www.change-management.com/tutorial-communications.htm

Chapter 16

Deane, Adam, *Business Process Quotes,* http://adamdeane.wordpress.com/2011/04/30/business-process-quotes/

Agile Deployment, http://www.centricsoftware.com/Resources/Files/Centric-8-PLM---Sourcing/DS_AGILE_Deployment_AUG2012_V03A.aspx

Deployment Flowchart, Wikipedia, http://en.wikipedia.org/wiki/Deployment_flowchart

Sinur, Jim, *Measuring The Cumulative Intelligence of a Process,* http://jimsinur.blogspot.ca/2013/05/measuring-cumulative-intelligence-of.html?m=1

Sinur, Jim, *First Test Drive of The Cumulative Process Intelligence Quotient,* http://jimsinur.blogspot.com/2013/05/first-test-drive-of-cumulative-process.html

Sinur, Jim, *Measuring The Autonomous Intelligence of Your Process Via Freedom Levels,* http://jimsinur.blogspot.com/2013/05/measuring-autonomous-intelligence-of.html

Sinur, Jim, *Visually Measuring The Cumulative Intelligence of Your Processes,* http://jimsinur.blogspot.com/2013/05/visually-measuring-cumulative.html

Sinur, Jim, *Measuring Levels of Raw Intelligence in Your Processes,* http://jimsinur.blogspot.com/2013/05/measuring-levels-of-raw-intelligence-in.html

Sinur, Jim, *Measuring The Social Intelligence of Your Processes,* http://jimsinur.blogspot.com/2013/05/measuring-social-intelligence-of-your.html

Process, http://www4.uwm.edu/cuts/bench/bm-desc.htm#Process:

The Benchmarking Process, http://www.nap.edu/openbook.php?record_id=11344&page=21

Gillen, David, *Benchmarking and Performance Measurement: The Role in Quality* Management, https://www.wlu.ca/documents/4293/Benchmarking.pdf

Chapter 17

Hunt, Julie, *From Tactical To Strategic Action: Operational Decision Management,* http://www.dataintegrationblog.com/data-quality/from-tactical-to-strategic-action-operational-decision-management-2/

Real-Time Interaction Management, http://www.information-management.com/infodirect/20000317/2034-1.html

Interaction Essential: What They Are, And Why They Matter, http://www.ddiworld.com/DDIWorld/media/monographs/interactionessentials_mg_ddi.pdf?ext=.pdf

Chapter 18

Deane, Adam, *Business Process Quotes,* http://adamdeane.wordpress.com/2011/04/30/business-process-quotes/

Business Process Management, http://en.wikipedia.org/wiki/Business_process_management#BPM_technology

Miers, Derek, *Reflections From a BPM Thought Leader: Alan Trefler, Pegasystems*

Chapter 19

Davenport, Tom, *10 Principle of The New Business Intelligence,* http://blogs.hbr.org/davenport/2008/12/10_principles_of_the_new_busin.html

Taylor, James, *James Taylor's Decision Management,* http://www.ebizq.net/blogs/decision_management/2008/07/decision_management_concept_4_1.php

Business Rules Platform, Pegasystems, http://www.pega.com/business-rules-platform

Business Rules, Pegasystems, http://www.pega.com/fr/business-rules

Pegasystems PegaRULES Process Commander V4 Makes Smart BPM Simpler To Develop, Manage and Use, http://www.pega.com/de/about-us/news-room/press-releases/pegasystems-pegarules-process-commander-v4-

makes-smart-bpm-simpler

John Reh, F, *Cross-Functional Teams Are a Way To Get Ahead*, http://management.about.com/od/careerdevelopment/a/Cross-Functional-Teams-Are-A-Way-To-Get-Ahead.htm

Managing Cross–Functional Teams, http://www.imanet.org/PDFs/Public/Research/SMA/Managing%20Cross%20Functional%20Teams.pdf

Kelchner, Luanne, *Strengths & Strengths of Cross Functional Teams,* http://smallbusiness.chron.com/strengths-weaknesses-cross-functional-teams-24653.html

Chapter 20

Suttle, Marilyn, *Quotable Quote*, Goodreads, http://www.goodreads.com/quotes/273220-after-each-customer-interaction-notice-if-you-gave-them-a

Govindarajan, Vijay, Srinivas, Srikanth, *When Your Incentive System Backfires,* http://blogs.hbr.org/cs/2013/02/when_your_incentive_system_backfires.html

Don, P, *4 Types of Customer Interactions To Plan For,* http://www.linkedin.com/today/post/article/20130114130809-17102372-4-types-of-customer-interactions-to-plan-for

Hoffman, Jody, Rogelberg, Steven, *A Guide To Team Incentive Systems,* http://orgscience.uncc.edu/sites/orgscience.uncc.edu/files/understanding%20team%20incentive%20systems.pdf

Luo, Xueming, Slotegraaf, J, Pan, Xing, *Cross-Functional "Coopetittion" The Simultaneous Role of Cooperation and Competition Within Firms,* http://wweb.uta.edu/faculty/luoxm/Home/jm.cross-function%20coop.luo.apr06.pdf

Profitability and Productivity Improvement – The Cross Functional Way, http://jlsears.squarespace.com/blog/2012/10/29/profitabilty-and-productivity-improvement-the-cross-function.html

Tregear, Roger, *Practical Process,* http://www.bptrends.com/publicationfiles/SEVEN%2012-09-COL-Practical%20Process-Practical%20Governance-Tregear%20rt-final.pdf

Rising, Linda, *Customer Interaction Patterns,* http://www.lcs.syr.edu/faculty/fawcett/handouts/CSE776/PatternPDFs/CustomerInteraction.pdf

Chapter 21

Process Quotes, http://www.brainyquote.com/quotes/keywords/process.html

Walker, Peter, *Is Predictive Analytics For The Future of BI?*, http://www.microscope.co.uk/opinion/Is-predictive-analytics-for-the-future-of-BI

Vaughan, Jack, *Predictive Analytics and Event Processing: The Future of BPM?*, http://searchsoa.techtarget.com/feature/Predictive-analytics-and-event-processing-The-future-of-BPM

McCarthy, Vance, *Pegasystems Unifies BPM, Rules, Predictive Analytics in Cloud, On-Premise*, http://www.idevnews.com/stories/4711/Pegasystems%20Unifies%20BPM,%20Rules,%20Predictive%20Analytics%20in%20Cloud,%20On-Premise

Spanyi, Andrew, Lojek, John, *Estimating and Demonstrating ROI on Business Process Management*, http://www.frontier-rt.com/drupal/sites/default/files/BPMROI_whitepaper_final_0.pdf

Griffin, Jane, *Developing Strategic KPI's For Your BPM System*, http://www.information-management.com/issues/20041001/1011033-1.html

Miers, Derek, Richardson, Clay, Cullen, Alex, Keenan, Julian, *Develop The Implementation Road Map For BPM Excellence*

Chapter 22

Operational Quotes, http://www.brainyquote.com/quotes/keywords/operational.html

Operational Intelligence: What It Is and Why You Need It Now, Splunk, http://www.splunk.com/web_assets/pdfs/secure/Why_You_Need_Operational_Intelligence.pdf

McCarthy, Vance, *Vitria Updates Operational Intelligence For Real Time Insights From Big Data, Events*, http://www.idevnews.com/stories/5681/Vitria-Updates-Operational-Intelligence-for-Real-Time-Insights-from-Big-Data-Events

Q & A: Operational Intelligence Delivers True Real Time Insights, http://tdwi.org/Articles/2012/10/30/Operational-Intelligence-Real-Time.aspx?Page=2

Business Activity Monitoring, Wikipedia, http://en.wikipedia.org/wiki/Business_activity_monitoring

Cosentino, Tony, *Like Big Data, Operational Intelligence is Evolving To Deliver Right Time Value,* http://tonycosentino.ventanaresearch.com/2013/01/02/like-big-data-operational-intelligence-is-evolving-to-deliver-right-time-value/

What Is Business Activity Monitoring?, http://publib.boulder.ibm.com/infocenter/dmndhelp/v6r2mx/index.jsp?topic=/com.ibm.btools.help.monitor.install.doc/intro/keyconcepts.html

Bruchey, Marchai, *Who Owns The Customer Experience?,* http://insights.wired.com/profiles/blogs/who-owns-the-customer-experience#axzz2V9BdAEbW

Q & A: Operational Intelligence Delivers True Real Time Insights, http://tdwi.org/Articles/2012/10/30/Operational-Intelligence-Real-Time.aspx?Page=2

Sharma, Manoj, *Role of Cross Functional Teams In Agile Projects,* http://www.projectdirectors.org/2013/02/cross-functional-teams-agile-projects.html

Carroll, Ian, *Agile Governance in a Nutshell,* http://iancarroll.com/2013/02/11/agile-governance-in-a-nutshell/

Agile Corporate Governance Aka Building a Lean Business You Can, http://xp2013.ideascale.com/a/dtd/378992-21177

Chapter 23

Optimization Quotes, http://www.brainyquote.com/quotes/keywords/optimization.html

George, Michael, *The Lean Six Sigma Guide To Doing More With Less,* http://www.accenture.com/SiteCollectionDocuments/PDF/Accenture_Lean_Six_Sigma.pdf

Khoshafian, Setrag, *2012: The Year of Doing More With Less (Part 2 of 2),* http://www.pega.com/nl/community/pega-blog/2012-the-year-of-doing-more-with-less-part-2-of-2

Brenner, Michael, *What Is Thought Leadership? 5 Steps To Get It Right,* http://www.forbes.com/sites/sap/2013/01/30/what-is-thought-leadership-5-steps-to-get-it-right/

Khoshafian, Setrag, *2012: The Year of Doing More With Less (Part 1 of 2)*, http://www.pega.com/community/pega-blog/2012-the-year-of-doing-more-with-less-part-1-of-2

The Power of Color, Pegasystems

Barnett, M, *Modeling & Simulation In Business Process Management*, http://bptrends.com/publicationfiles/11-03%20WP%20Mod%20Simulation%20of%20BPM%20-%20Barnett-1.pdf

Massias, Mark, Dr, *How Intersystems Technology Enables Business Intelligence Solutions*, http://www.intersystems.com/ensemble/whitepapers/pdf/BIS.pdf

About the Author

When it comes to driving strategic goals, more revenue, and people, Jason Miller certainly has enough experience. With more than 12 years of experience with business operations and business technology, Jason Miller has the unique professional ability to translate business strategy into effective implementation.

In addition to taking on his new role as author, he currently is responsible for strategic initiatives surrounding process standardization for Decisioning and Advanced Analytics with Fortune 500 Telecommunication Services Provider.

Jason's talent is for managing and leading large-scale programs that are customer experience driven. His approach integrates people, processes, and technology to deliver a result of successful change. His list of accomplishments over the course of his 12+ years working in the field is lengthy and continues to grow.

For one thing, Jason has demonstrated his abilities to lead multiple team projects, thrive in the field of technology development, process design, and analyze as well as interact and change management. He carries out all of this utilizing his consulting approach. Plus his ability to define goals and achieve them with excellence makes him an expert in his field.

This important knowledge Jason now shares with his readers in *Intelligent Interactions: Practical Guide To Profitable Customer Experience*. This will enable readers to, among many other things, take on the duty of establishing a long-term Interaction Center of Excellence for their own organization. This comprehensive guide gives you the knowledge and insight Jason has spent more than 12 years gathering so that you, too, can become an expert.

www.ingramcontent.com/pod-product-compliance
Lightning Source LLC
Chambersburg PA
CBHW051634170526
45167CB00001B/191